WOLF

WOLF

Maureen Greeley

BARNES
&NOBLE
BOOKS
NEW YORK

This edition published by Barnes & Noble, Inc.
by arrangement with Michael Friedman Publishing Group, Inc.

1997 Barnes & Noble Books

ISBN 0-7607-0547-X

M 10 9 8 7 6 5 4 3

Editor: Susan Lauzau
Art Director: Jeff Batzli
Designer: Andrea Karman
Photography Editor: Samantha Larrance
Illustrations by: Pat Ortega

Color separations by Bright Arts (Singapore) Pte. Ltd.
Printed and bound in China by Leefung-Asco Printers Ltd.

DEDICATION

To those who recognize the fragile threads that connect all life in a wondrous woven whole.

To those whose lives and spirits have inspired in me and in others a childlike awe of the natural world, a reverence that can never be diminished.

To those whose support and encouragement have oftentimes made the difference between pulling back and reaching for higher stars.

To my parents, my sister, and my husband—and all my family of friends—for sharing these joys.

To Little John, Kiowa, Lucan, Clementine, Morning Star, Cris, Joshua, Tahoma, Destiny, Moose, and so many other wolves who daily remind me of a wisdom humans cannot fully comprehend and of the hope I hear in their every song.

With great thanks and respect for all of you, I dedicate this book to a wise and gentle friend...

FOR CAILE

Contents

Wolves Majestic and Maligned

THROUGH THE CENTURIES,

WE HAVE PROJECTED

ONTO THE WOLF

THE QUALITIES WE MOST DESPISE AND FEAR

IN OURSELVES.

—BARRY LOPEZ, *OF WOLVES AND MEN*

Destiny, perhaps from the very beginning, claimed the wolf as a symbol. Has any other animal stirred human passions the way the wolf has? Its haunting howl, its incredible stamina, its brilliant eyes, and its superiority as a predator all have been reviled as nefarious, and even demonic, traits. Ironically, these same characteristics have also been revered as belonging to a majestic, and sometimes spiritual, creature—a symbol of the magnificent, untamed wilderness.

In truth, the wolf is neither evil nor exceptionally good—neither demon nor god. Wolves are simply predators. Their role as predator must not be reduced, however, to that of savage killer. Wolves, like humans, need to eat to survive. In this process, wolves also provide a service: they help preserve nature's delicate balance by keeping herds of deer, elk, moose, and other large mammals in check, as well as keeping these populations strong and genetically viable by preying on the weak and sick.

Both the idealized wolf and the demonic wolf are creations of the human mind. It is not easy to transcend the image of the Big Bad Wolf that has filled our myths and legends, but if we know only this wolf we do not truly know the wolf at all. And what we do not know, we fear. Our fear is perhaps the greatest threat to the survival of the wolf, for it causes us to react rather than act, to repel rather than respect. But this fear and hatred did not always separate man and beast.

Man the hunter once looked on wolf the hunter with admiration. Man and wolf both used their keen intelligence to overcome the disadvantages they faced in their day-to-day existence. Survival for both was enhanced by hunting and living in groups or packs. And, at one time, the chance of survival for each was also increased by following, learning from, and adapting the skills of the other to its own advantage.

As long as man's daily living was earned primarily as a hunter, he knew a respect for wolves, and coexistence was relatively peaceful. Eventually, man and wolf took up together in a process of domestication that brought a different meaning to their coexistence.

Even while those early ancestors of man's best friend enjoyed this new relationship, the wolves that did not come in from the cold were beginning to be cast in a different and less favorable light, for the dog was not the only animal toward whom man turned his attention in the early days of animal husbandry. Some ten thousand years ago, man discovered great value for himself in domesticating animals such as cattle and sheep—it was far easier to herd sufficient numbers of animals to supply adequate food than to hunt them.

Man left the forest for the field, and the wilderness became a vast and frightening entity. While the domesticated dog was soon pressed into service to guard these herds of goats, cattle, and sheep, his cousin the wolf was now seen as a threat and an enemy. The wolf, again a symbol, stood not for a majestic, bountiful wilderness, but rather for a foreign, untamed wilderness that must be conquered.

ABOVE: Benevolent wolf mothers who bring up human children are found in the mythology of several cultures. Among the famous "wolf children" are Romulus and Remus, the legendary founders of Rome. These twin sons of the god Mars and a vestal virgin were banished at birth and condemned to death, but their cries fell on the ears of a wolf mother who suckled them. Romulus and Remus lived to restore their grandfather, Numitor, as ruler of Alba; their tale lived on to spawn other stories of children raised by wolves.

The Big Bad Wolf

With the spread of Christianity, the Bible's injunction to subdue and conquer the earth spread through the forests with the intensity and destructiveness of a fire as man declared war on the wolf. The wolf was particularly nefarious in the folklore, literature, and Church teachings of medieval Europe. Still influenced by the ignorance and superstitions of the Dark Ages, and only beginning to reach toward the enlightenment of the Renaissance, medieval man was fraught with fears, not the least of which was theriophobia.

Theriophobia, literally, is fear of animals. In his book *Of Wolves and Men*, noted author and editor Barry Lopez explains theriophobia as: "Fear of the beast. Fear of the beast as an irrational, violent, insatiable creature.

Fear of the projected beast in oneself....At the heart of theriophobia is the fear of one's own nature. In its headiest manifestations theriophobia is projected onto a single animal, the animal becomes a scapegoat, and it is annihilated."

It is true that wolves in the Middle Ages, like foxes, skunks, and even domestic and feral dogs, sometimes carried and transmitted rabies, a terrible disease that we, fortunately, almost never encounter today. Rabies was always fatal. Still, great legends of evil skunks, foxes, or dogs did not follow these animals as they did the wolf. Indeed, man's fear of wolves clearly bordered on hysteria during this time, fomented by tales of wicked creatures acting out of allegiance to the darkest powers of hell.

ABOVE: Little Red Riding Hood is among the most compelling cautionary tales in Western culture. Its impact is unquestionable in perpetuating the myth of the Big Bad Wolf. **PAGE 14:** *Top left:* The most frightening mythical representation of the wolf is the terrifying transformation of man into beast in the form of a werewolf. The first film dramatization of the subject, *The Werewolf*, was produced in 1913. One of the most recent variations on the theme, starring Jack Nicholson in the title role, was called simply *Wolf*. *Top right:* The very characteristics that elicit fear of the wolf are the ones that help wolves keep peace within the pack. While many people would see the message conveyed by this snarling wolf as a threat of aggression, the ears laid back indicate a greater sense of fear than in the more dominant wolf below. *Bottom left:* This striking black wolf's clear communication—with ears erect and gaze intense—is likely to settle an argument before any further physical action becomes necessary. The highly focused gaze of the wolf is a characteristic that makes many people uncomfortable. In an interesting twist on man/wolf transformation tales, the Bella Coola Indians believed that someone once tried to transform all the animals into men, but was successful in making human only the eyes of the wolf. *Bottom right:* Perhaps the ultimate portrayal of a werewolf was Lon Chaney's in the 1941 movie *The Wolf Man*. The common thread that runs through all the movies and stories of werewolves may have less to do with the nature of wolves than with the nature of human beings. **PAGE 15:** The size of the ears, eyes, nose, and teeth on this wolf head effigy, which dates from A.D. 800–1400, shows how clearly the wolf's use of its keen senses were recognized by the artist.

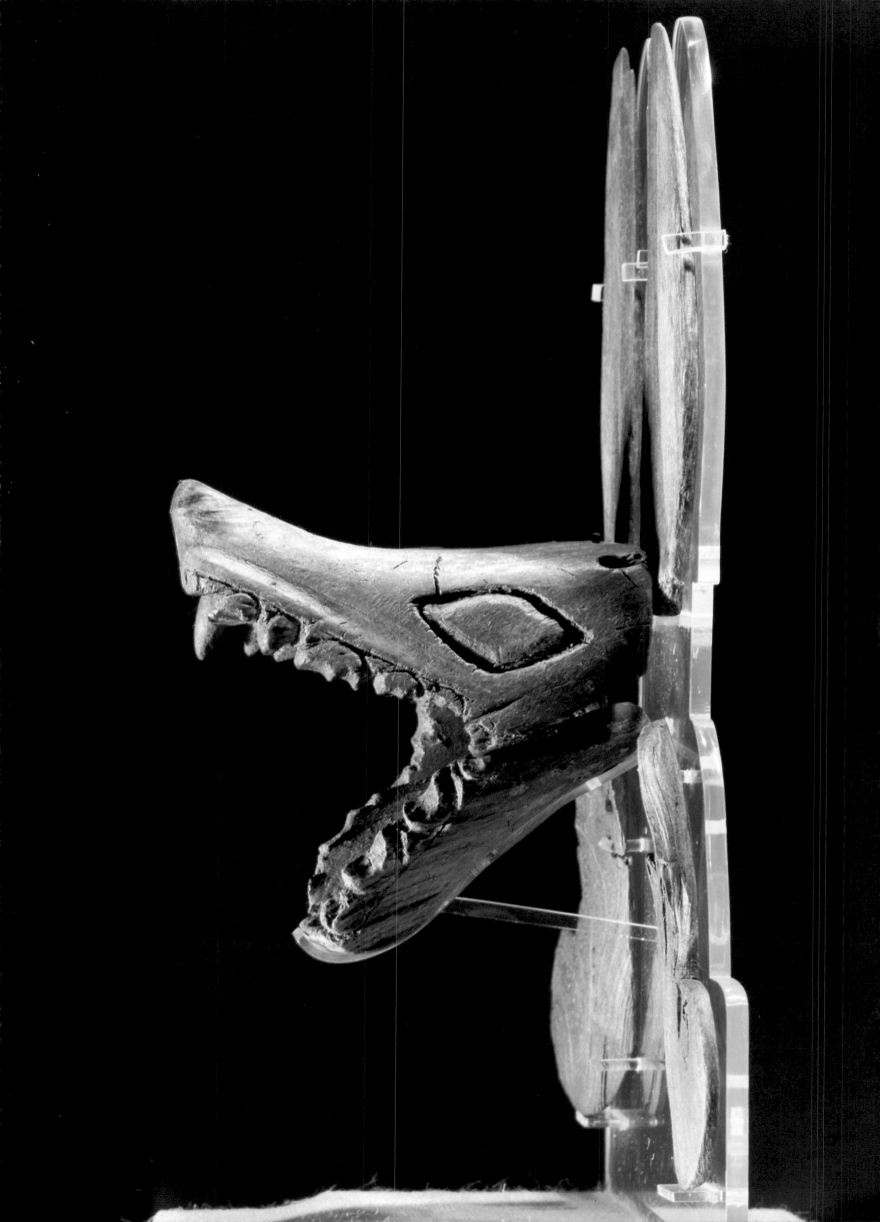

Even worse than the wolf was the human-wolf creature known as the werewolf. That man could take on an evil animal form to attack, kill, and sometimes devour other humans struck fear in the hearts and minds of medieval man. Only the fears of facing the court of the Inquisition were greater. It was during this time of intimidation and hysteria that werewolves became brethren to witches and sorcerers. Brother was set against brother and sister against sister as accusations of possession by these evil forces flew. Each feared lest he find himself the object of this terrifying witch hunt.

The wolf in most legends and fairy tales is a vicious, devious killer. Whether these stories sought to portray the wolf itself or simply to reflect the beast within our own nature, they did nothing to promote a positive relationship between wolves and men.

Another facet of wolf legend told of the kindly female wolf who nursed the legendary founders of Rome. These baby twins, named Romulus and Remus, were the illegitimate sons of a vestal virgin and the god Mars. Condemned to death and cast into the Tiber River, they washed ashore and their cries were answered by a

ABOVE: The wolf is not always characterized as menacing in literature. In Rudyard Kipling's classic tale *The Jungle Book*, baby Mowgli is adopted by a family of wolves in the jungles of India. Mowgli experiences a life of adventures no human has ever known. His friends and teachers in the animal kingdom help him learn about life in the jungle, but can't help him learn about his own kind or find his place in the world. Kipling wrote this exciting and imaginative tale in 1894 for his daughter, Josephine. **OPPOSITE:** Keeping the wolf at bay is the theme of this engraving. Its original caption read: "I snatched the poker from the fire, and, armed with the iron at white heat, I proceeded to wolf number one."

female wolf. She cared for them and nursed them, eventually placing them in a cave where a shepherd found them and took them into his own family.

In Rudyard Kipling's classic tale *The Jungle Book*, infant Mowgli is adopted by a family of wolves in the jungles of India. From them and from other animals Mowgli learns the laws of the jungle and experiences a life no other human has ever known.

These wonderful stories were clearly intended to teach people about themselves rather than about the nature of wolves. Tales of human infants brought up by wolves as members of their pack cross many geographical and cultural boundaries, though none can be authenticated.

Wolves in the New World, in particular, posed little physical threat to humans, as the wide-open spaces meant that there was little contact between the two species. Still, early American settlers brought with them the fear of wolves that was so entrenched in European culture. They also brought an even stronger and more overriding belief—that man should have dominion over all other creatures, and over the land as well. Puritan ministers of the eighteenth century, including Cotton Mather, enjoined members of their congregations to destroy the evil wilderness as a sign of their religious fervor and commitment to the Lord, to make of the "howling wilderness a fruitful field." A cash bounty on wolves was established in Plymouth Colony as early as 1630. Within ten years, the increasing bounty payment of forty shillings per wolf was equal to a month's wages for a laborer.

In the nineteenth century, this mandate to dominate the wild combined with the surge west, further complicating man's relationship with the wolf. The principles of Manifest Destiny lured settlers across the Great Plains and over the Rockies with the guarantee of fertile land to farm and open grassland for grazing sheep and cattle. But the promise of prosperity for man meant certain persecution for the wolf. Displaced from their former wide range, wolves retreated to smaller and smaller areas. Perceived as a threat to both livestock and humans, the wolf was systematically eradicated through hunting and poisoning.

WOLF WORDS TO LIVE BY

In many cases the legendary villainy of the wolf has been concentrated into a few morals or proverbs by which man could live his life:

"Beware of the wolf in sheep's clothing" warned of dangerous trickery.

"Keeping the wolf from the door" referred to warding off starvation or creditors.

We are admonished to "never cry wolf," for giving false alarm of danger will always bring trouble upon our heads.

And, the most repugnant— to "throw someone to the wolves"—implies sacrificing another's life to save yourself.

A Wolf Tale

Stories handed down from generation to generation on through the oral tradition grow richer through retelling. The fables of Aesop were part of that oral tradition and were most likely written down over time by several different authors. In many of these collected fables, the wolf has a starring role—often as a fierce, greedy, selfish, and wicked tyrant.

The best known of the numerous fables featuring the wolf are "The Boy Who Cried Wolf" and "The Wolf in Sheep's Clothing." Fewer people recognize immediately such fables as "The Wolf and His Shadow," "The Mother and the Wolf," and "The Wolf and the Shepherd." One of these lesser-known stories, "The Dog and the Wolf," is retold here. In this story the wolf is a somewhat more sympathetic and even noble character, who rejects domestication and reasserts his own wild nature.

THE DOG AND THE WOLF

There was once a forlorn Wolf who had had little to eat for many days. He had grown very thin and very tired. His coat was sparse, and winter was approaching. One evening the sad and weary Wolf had a very unusual encounter with a fine and obviously well fed Dog wandering near edge of the village by the woods.

Surprised and impressed, the Wolf remarked at how shiny the Dog's coat appeared, and how much energy he had.

"You, too, can look so fine and eat so well," encouraged the Dog.

Eager to eat, the Wolf asked how.

"Life in the woods is far too hard," said the Dog. "Leave the woods behind and come with me and you shall never have to hunt and fight for your food again."

The Wolf was skeptical, but his curiosity was piqued, and he asked just what the Dog did in return for such splendor and comfort.

"Very little," replied the Dog. "I protect my master's house from thieves, although there never have been any, and I curl up at his feet when I'm allowed. For this I have sumptuous scraps from the table—bits of chicken and lamb, beef and bread, kind words, and a place to rest my head."

The tired Wolf, his stomach growling, was filled with visions of an easy life and a full stomach, and nearly sprang to his feet to follow the Dog when something caught his eye.

"What is this strange marking around your neck?" asked the Wolf, noticing a band of skin where the Dog's fur had been worn away.

"That's nothing," answered the Dog.

"Nothing?" questioned the Wolf.

"You see simply the mark from my collar and chain. I hardly notice it myself any more. It means little."

"Little!" the Wolf cried. "Are you not free to roam at will when and where you please?"

"Only when I slip away, but not very often," said the Dog. "At night, they chain me to a tree, but my kennel is close at hand in case it rains. I've no complaints."

The Wolf could not believe his ears. "A chain! A kennel! I'd have complaints," he cried. "I may be cold and wet some nights and I may know hunger well, but my freedom is one thing, good friend, that I will never sell!"

The Wolf turned away, still hungry but no longer forlorn or weary.

A sadder and wiser Dog watched him trot away.

There is nothing so valuable in life as freedom.

Native American Perceptions of the Wolf

Native American traditions and understandings of nature were very different from those that Europeans brought with them.

By and large, the different Native American cultures shared a respect for other creatures. When a person needed the qualities best represented by a certain animal, he or she asked or prayed for them. Many Native American peoples called the wolf the Pathfinder or Teacher, and admired wolves as intelligent, courageous, and strong. They also saw in the wolf a loyal pack member who provided for the community as a whole whenever necessary. The stories about wolves handed down from generation to generation are predominantly tales of wolf the keen hunter, wolf the devoted family member, wolf the proud defender of his territory, wolf the intelligent teacher, and wolf the true survivor. These were characteristics deserving of great respect and emulation. To carry wolf power, among many tribes, was to be greatly honored. In turn, the wolf was honored in ceremony and legend, and in dance and song.

Perceptions of wolves differed between Native American cultures that relied heavily on hunting and those that were primarily agricultural. The wolf, after all, is a great hunter who moves smoothly and almost silently over plains or through forests. It was for the hunter or the shaman that the wolf played the greatest role, rather than for the farmer.

The Navajo, however, called the wolf *mai-coh,* a synonym for witch. Their fear of wolves, like that of so many Europeans, was based not on the nature of the wolf, but on human nature. Both the Navajo and the Hopi believed that human witches used (or even abused) the wolf's powers to harm other people. While Europeans warned of a wolf in sheep's clothing, certain tribal beliefs cautioned against a human in wolf's clothing. The powers of the wolf in Native American belief, then, could be called upon and used by humans for good or bad.

The wolf—the symbolic wolf—has at various times and places been the focus of great respect and honor and at others the recipient of hatred and persecution. Can we put aside the legends and learn to live with the true wolf and all wildlife? The wolf is a survivor—but for how long? If the wolf is to avoid extinction, we, as stewards of the earth, must let go of our fears. We must strive to understand that every living creature has its purpose and value, and we must learn to recognize the balance and beauty of nature. Then, and only then, will the wolf's true destiny emerge.

ABOVE: This Native American wooden dance hat, collected on the Northwest coast of the United States in 1879, has a wolf on its crest. Such stylized representations of wolves were common on masks, totem poles, and headpieces like this one. Sacred white eagle down was concealed in a hollow inside the potlatch rings attached to the hat and was scattered by the jerking head movements of the ceremonial dancer, ensuring goodwill.

The wolves and Plains Indians of North America shared their hunting territories, a practice that was documented by artist George Catlin in his paintings. Several well-known pieces from 1832 to 1833 recorded the importance of wolves in this culture: the paintings *White Wolves Attacking a Buffalo* and *Buffalo Hunt Under the Wolf-Skin Mask* depict the keen hunting skills learned from the wolves. This piece, *Crow Lodge of Twenty-Five Buffalo Skins*, shows the wolf in a more domestic relationship with the Plains Indians.

A Brave New World for Wolves

Throughout the twentieth century, and now at the brink of the twenty-first, the myth of the wolf as villain has been perpetuated. The first werewolf movie was made as early as 1913. Known simply as *The Werewolf*, it was followed over the years by such movies as *The Wolf Man, Curse of the Werewolf, Teen Wolf, The Howling, An American Werewolf in London*, and, most recently, *Wolf*.

Though both a title character and a positive one in *Dances with Wolves* and *Never Cry Wolf*, these are rare roles for the wolf. In the former movie, a tentative but respectful relationship grows between the hero and a wolf (which is later killed). *Never Cry Wolf*, both a book and a movie, is entertaining and highly romanticized, but did succeed in evoking a newfound sympathy for wolves and in chipping away at centuries-old stereotypes.

But it is in documentaries, contemporary nonfiction, and art that the true wolf is beginning to emerge, and it is through these modern representations that we may finally reach an understanding of and with the wolf.

TOP: A friendly muzzle lick is part of the greeting ritual expressed by a subordinate wolf to a more dominant pack member. **ABOVE:** Though wolves are known for their speed and agility in the hunt, they can also show great patience and silent stalking skills when approaching prey. **OVERLEAF:** More than any other canid, wolves are social animals. From the time they are pups, they spend nearly all their time in the company of other wolves. Cooperation is vital to the survival of the pack because life in the wild is hard.

Chapter 2

Wild Dogs— Domestic Dogs

WE NEED ANOTHER AND A WISER, PERHAPS A MORE MYSTICAL, CONCEPT OF ANIMALS. REMOTE FROM UNIVERSAL NATURE AND LIVING BY COMPLICATED ARTIFICE, MAN IN CIVILIZATION SURVEYS THE CREATURE THROUGH THE GLASS OF HIS KNOWLEDGE AND SEES THEREBY A FEATHER MAGNIFIED AND THE WHOLE IMAGE IN DISTORTION. WE PATRONIZE THEM FOR THEIR INCOMPLETENESS, FOR THEIR TRAGIC FATE OF HAVING TAKEN FORM SO FAR BELOW OURSELVES. AND THEREIN WE ERR, AND GREATLY ERR. FOR THE ANIMAL SHALL NOT BE MEASURED BY MAN. IN A WORLD OLDER AND MORE COMPLETE THAN OURS THEY MOVE FINISHED AND COMPLETE, GIFTED WITH EXTENSIONS OF THE SENSES WE HAVE LOST OR NEVER ATTAINED, LIVING BY VOICES WE SHALL NEVER HEAR. THEY ARE NOT BRETHREN. THEY ARE NOT UNDERLINGS. THEY ARE OTHER NATIONS—CAUGHT WITH OURSELVES IN THE NET OF LIFE AND TIME, FELLOW PRISONERS OF THE SPLENDOR AND TRAVAIL OF THE EARTH.

—HENRY BESTON

Evolution and the Ecological Niche

Wolf tracks crossed the great expanses of the Northern Hemisphere long before man's first footprint made its mark. Though the first true wolves appeared only about one million years ago, their story certainly doesn't begin there.

When the reign of the dinosaurs came to an end some sixty-five million years ago, at the close of the Cretaceous period, there was a noticeable lack of large predatory species in the fossil record. With increasing specialization, a small, tree-climbing creature called *Miacis* emerged about fifty million years ago as the progenitor not only of wolves and other canids, but of several other meat eaters, including bears and raccoons.

From *Miacis* evolved a more distinctive protocanid known as *Hesperocyon*. Short of limb with a weasellike body, *Hesperocyon* showed more wolflike characteristics than *Miacis*; it boasted a long tail, the habit of walking on its toes, and a longer muzzle that accommodated forty-two teeth.

Primitive canids continued to evolve, and around twenty-five to thirty million years ago, the ancestors of today's wild dogs emerged. *Cynodesmus* had not only a long tail, but long legs compared to other canids. Its thin, retractable claws were more like those of a cat.

By Miocene times, twenty million years ago, cats and dogs each comprised their own distinct superfamily of carnivores. Cats, with their stealth, were well suited to the forest and jungle, and were masters at the art of ambushing their prey. Dogs found their evolutionary niche as climatic changes saw previously wooded areas replaced by open

grassland. Long legs and incredible stamina allowed these canids to pace themselves in pursuit of prey and as they journeyed across the Bering land bridge from America to Asia and, eventually, into Europe.

The Bering land bridge, or lack of it, played a significant role in the evolution of animal populations, including the canids. During the Pleistocene epoch, which began some one to one and a half million years ago, this land bridge, spanning what is now the Bering Strait, appeared and disappeared as ice ages and thaws caused water and ice levels to rise and fall. The Bering land bridge represented a vital link between the American and Eurasian continents. When it made an appearance, animal populations took advantage of the opportunity to move back and forth between the continents. After the bridge again disappeared these now isolated animals evolved uniquely to fit their new environments.

This era of ice ages produced impressive "giants," from incredible bison with horns ten feet (3m) long to mastodons and woolly mammoths. It also produced an impressive array of predators that met the challenges presented by their massive prey. This was the era of saber-toothed tigers, hulking bears, and dire wolves. These oversized wolves had massive skulls with immense teeth and powerful jaws.

The discovery of more than two thousand dire wolves mired in the La Brea tar pits near Los Angeles, California, sheds some light not only on their size and form, but also on their feeding habits. The bubbling oil that began to surface at this site some forty thousand years ago left a thick layer

of tar as the liquid evaporated. Falling leaves and twigs covered the tar, making the sticky surface appear solid.

Animals, including many herbivores such as bison, ground sloths, and horses, were attracted to the pools that were created where hollows in the tar pits filled with water. The attraction proved deadly, as these animals became mired in the sticky tar. A similar attraction also proved deadly for eager carrion-feeding scavengers such as dire wolves, who found the large numbers of their prey trapped at the tar pits irresistible and so became stuck themselves.

As wolves continued to evolve, the imposing dire wolf eventually became extinct, but the wolf—in the form of *Canis lupus*, the gray wolf we know today—remained the largest member of the dog family and, for many years, also had the widest range of any land mammal. The wolf's massive and varied range encompassed a large part of the Northern Hemisphere in both the Old and New Worlds, where it thrived in all but the most arid deserts, the tallest mountains, and tropical forests.

The ecological niche to which the wolf is so well suited is that of preeminent predator upon large mammals in the Northern Hemisphere. The only other animals that regu-

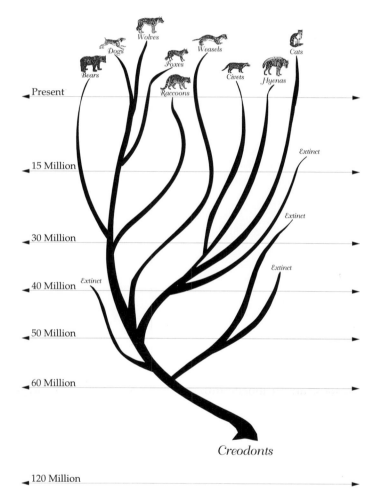

TOP, FROM LEFT TO RIGHT: *Miacis, Hesperocyon,* and *Cynodesmus* are three prehistoric carnivores that played an integral part in the wolf's evolution. **ABOVE RIGHT:** Some sixty million years ago, in the Paleocene, the ancestors of the wolf began to develop. They found a niche as carnivores that hunted by chasing their prey. As these creatures evolved, they developed partially retractable claws and long, thick tails. As climatic changes took place, some of these carnivores moved out of the forests and onto the plains, giving rise to bears, raccoons, weasels, and wolves. Those carnivores that continued to inhabit the trees took a separate evolutionary path—retaining their retractable claws and refining an ambush style of hunting—and their descendants survive as members of the cat family.

larly prey on large mammals in the Northern Hemisphere are members of the cat family (Felidae)—represented by the cougar or mountain lion and jaguar in North America, and by leopards, lions, and tigers in Asia—and, of course, humans.

As the last ice age melted away and once-frozen areas of the north became forested, human hunters might, understandably, have appreciated the unique qualities that made the wolf a skillful hunter, particularly its ability to run down its prey and its enhanced senses of smell and hearing. Wary wolves might scavenge what man left behind from his hunts, discovering an easier and less dangerous way to feed. By the same token, a band of human hunters who stumbled on a successful wolf kill might have given in to the temptation to chase the

wolves away from a hard-won meal. But the alliance between man and wolf would develop slowly.

Early wolves and humans guarded their territory carefully. As wolves became somewhat habituated to humans, they began to play a vital role in defending the homesite against intruders, both two-legged and four-legged. Rewards of food and shelter were, apparently, enough for some to give up the freedom of the wild.

Whatever their reasons, sometime between ten thousand and fifteen thousand years ago, wolves and humans made the first efforts to hunt and work together. Little could our ancestors and the ancestors of our domestic dogs have understood what this relationship would mean or how it would evolve in the centuries to come.

Dire wolves challenge a saber-toothed cat for a mammoth that has succumbed to the sticky tar of the La Brea tar pits. Unfortunately for the wolves and the cat, the tar pits will also claim them as victims. The fossil remains found at this site near Los Angeles, California, tell an interesting story. Two types of animal are common: large herbivores such as bison, ground sloths, and horses that grazed the surrounding plains were attracted by the hundreds to pools of water at the surface, and far larger numbers of carnivores, undoubtedly attracted by what seemed easy prey, were also trapped. The bones of more than one thousand saber-toothed cats and more than fifteen hundred dire wolves have been found here.

The Family Canidae

The wolf's extended family—the family Canidae—includes foxes, jackals, domestic dogs, dingoes, dholes, and bush dogs and other wild dogs. The Canidae as a whole are related most closely to the bears (family Ursidae) and, on a more distant level, to other carnivores, such as civets, raccoons, weasels, and even cats and hyenas. While wolves, dingoes, domestic dogs, and jackals are all grouped together in the genus *Canis,* most of the foxes are classified in the genus *Vulpes.* Though we often use the word "canine" to refer to a domestic dog, all animals in the genus *Canis* are canines.

So what distinguishes canines from other animals? While every characteristic is not absolute among all canines, they do share a great number of traits. Wolves, coyotes, foxes, and many wild dogs, for instance, all have relatively long legs. Even domestic dogs—whether long or short of limb—share with other canines their blunt, nonretractable claws and four-toed feet (a fifth toe on each of the front feet exists as a dew claw).

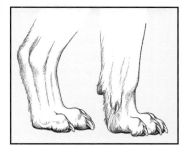

Most canines have elongated skulls and jaws to accommodate their forty-two teeth (including the impressive canine teeth, which bear the name of the genus). Unlike their domesticated cousins, wild canines are generally shy and elusive, and can produce only one litter of young per year. A long, thick coat with several layers of hair, a bushy tail, and specialized scent glands at the base of the tail are also distinctive to canines. Most important, perhaps, is that canines are highly intelligent, and many are also highly social.

This sociability depends somewhat on the hunting styles of the particular species and on the availability of certain types of prey. Wolves, for instance, depend on pack stability and cooperation to successfully bring down large prey such as deer, moose, and wapiti; when big game is scarce, large packs break down into smaller groups to hunt less impressive prey. In contrast, foxes normally prey on smaller animals such as small birds and rodents, and often live a fairly solitary life.

TOP: The wolf looks much like a large dog, and in fact, domestic dogs are descended from wolves. The gray wolf's legs are much longer than a dog's, however, and its feet are larger. As it walks, the wolf's hind feet step into the pawprints of its front feet, gaining a distinct advantage in traveling through snow; its narrow chest, too, is efficient for plowing through deep drifts. **ABOVE:** Each back paw (left) has four toes; each front paw (right) is larger than a back paw and has four toes plus a dew claw.

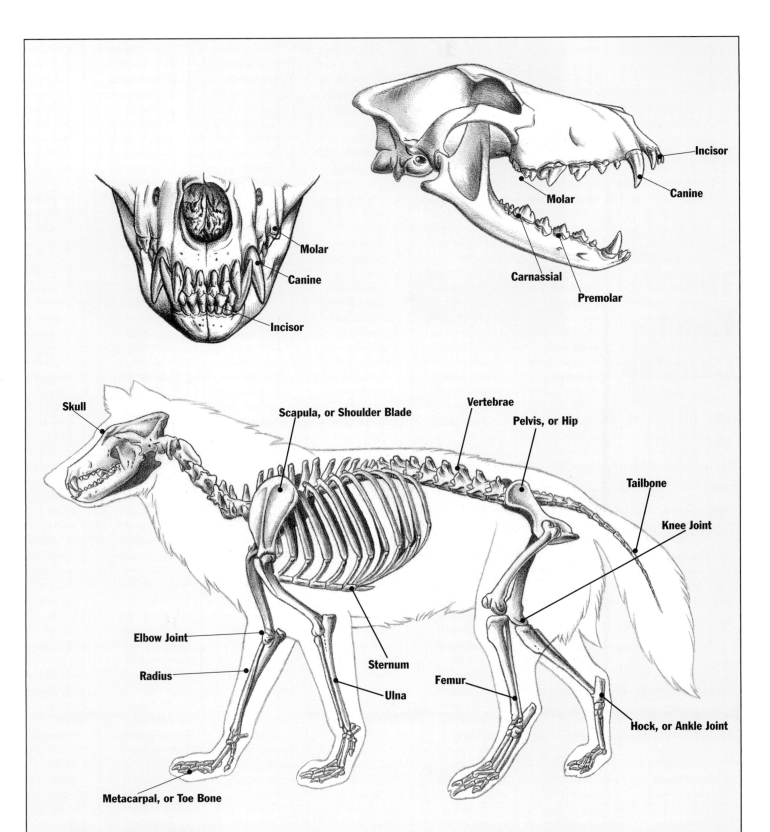

Molar

Canine

Incisor

Incisor

Canine

Molar

Carnassial

Premolar

Skull

Scapula, or Shoulder Blade

Vertebrae

Pelvis, or Hip

Tailbone

Knee Joint

Elbow Joint

Radius

Sternum

Ulna

Femur

Hock, or Ankle Joint

Metacarpal, or Toe Bone

TOP, LEFT AND RIGHT: The canine teeth, which may reach two inches (5cm) in length, can pierce through thick hide and are used to hold prey, while incisors, located at the front of the jaw, tear flesh from bones. Premolars and molars are used to both cut and grind. The carnassial teeth, which are larger than surrounding teeth, are specially adapted for slicing flesh rather than tearing. Molars at the back of the mouth pulverize bones and other hard material. **ABOVE:** The wolf's skeleton shows it to be supremely adapted to life in the wild: its thick skull protects the brain, eyes, nose, and ears, and accommodates the many teeth; strong ribs safeguard delicate internal organs; and long limbs are ideal for speed.

Family Album

A wolf pup raises its voice and announces its presence to the world. Helpless at birth, by the age of four to five weeks, pups are ready to explore the vast world outside their den.

GRAY WOLF

Canis lupus

DISTRIBUTION: The gray wolf's once-extensive range included a great part of the Northern Hemisphere, with the exception of arid deserts and tropical forests. Its current range is more restricted but includes parts of North America, areas within some European countries, and select ranges in Asia.

DESCRIPTION: The largest member of the canid family, the gray wolf may reach up to six feet (1.8m) in length (including the tail), and stands from thirty-three to thirty-eight inches (84 to 96.5 cm) high at the shoulder. Average weight ranges from seventy to one hundred pounds (32 to 45kg); females are generally smaller than males. Size varies through its range; animals in colder climates have larger, bulkier bodies to help them conserve heat. As its name implies, the gray wolf's coat appears in many shades of gray; it may also range from white to black with many combinations in between, including cream, tan, buff, sandy brown, and reddish.

SOCIABILITY: Highly social. The size of the pack varies from fewer than seven to twenty, depending partly on availability of prey.

OFFSPRING: Gray wolves breed once a year, around January or February, depending on the latitude; gestation is sixty-three days, with litters of typically five or six pups born between March and May.

PREY/DIET: Moose, deer, elk, caribou, bison, beaver, rabbits, and mice are the main prey of the gray wolf.

STATUS: Protected under the Endangered Species Act in the United States (except in Alaska, where they are not endangered), gray wolves are listed as endangered in forty-seven of the lower forty-eight states; in Minnesota they are listed as threatened. Protection varies in Canada, Asia, and Europe from full protection to game status for hunting; in some areas bounties for killed wolves are still offered.

RED WOLF

Canis rufus

Some scientists believe that the red wolf should be regarded as a subspecies of the gray wolf, *Canis lupus*; recent genetic analysis has raised some doubts about the validity of the red wolf as a separate species.

DISTRIBUTION: Though the red wolf once ranged from coasts of Florida and Georgia to central Texas, and along the Mississippi River valley from the Gulf of Mexico into central Missouri and southern Illinois, it now exists only in reintroduced populations in North Carolina and Tennessee. It is the top canine predator of the southeastern forests of the United States.

DESCRIPTION: The red wolf weighs approximately thirty-three to eighty pounds (15 to 36kg), stands about twenty-eight inches (71cm) at the shoulder, and measures an average of fifty-five inches (140cm) from tip of nose to end of tail. The coat of the red wolf shows considerable variation, from copper to cinnamon with deep gray-brown and black highlights. Fur on the underparts is generally lighter.

SOCIABILITY: The red wolf lives in small family packs that average two to eight members.

OFFSPRING: Red wolves breed once a year, with pups born after a sixty-one- to sixty-three-day gestation.

PREY/DIET: Red wolves feed on nutria, raccoons, deer, rabbits, squirrels, and some birds.

STATUS: Almost extinct in the wild, the red wolf has recently been reintroduced into Tennessee and northeastern parts of North Carolina.

When is a Wolf Not a Wolf?

AARDWOLF
Proteles cristatus

Aardwolf is an Afrikaans word meaning "earth wolf," though the aardwolf is not a wolf at all, but rather a member of the family Hyaenidae. The Swahili name for the aardwolf is *fisi ndogo*, or "little hyena."

DISTRIBUTION: The dry brush country of southern and eastern Africa, including parts of Kenya, Uganda, Namibia, and Angola, is home to the aardwolf.

DESCRIPTION: The aardwolf's forequarters are higher than its rear, and its height at the shoulder is seventeen and a half to twenty inches (44.5 to 51cm). Vertical dark bands stand out against the aardwolf's tawny coat. A bushy mane runs from neck to tail.

SOCIABILITY: The aardwolf is almost entirely nocturnal and often solitary, though pairs and family groups of five or six animals are sometimes seen.

OFFSPRING: Aardwolves bear litters of two to four young. Several females may share a den.

PREY/DIET: The aardwolf feeds mainly on termites and insect larvae.

MANED WOLF
Chrysocyon brachyurus

The maned wolf is actually a South American wild dog, and is more closely related to foxes than to wolves.

DISTRIBUTION: The maned wolf inhabits the grassy plains, forest borders, and edges of swamps in eastern parts of South America, including areas of Argentina, Bolivia, Brazil, and Uruguay.

DESCRIPTION: Up to thirty inches (76cm) at the shoulder with long, slender legs and large ears, its average weight is forty-five pounds (20.5kg). Long reddish fur with distinctive black markings on the muzzle, legs, and back characterize the maned wolf. The tip of its tail and chin may be white.

SOCIABILITY: Solitary and nocturnal, pairs share a territory but come together infrequently except to breed. Both parents help rear pups, alternating duties between pup-sitting and hunting.

OFFSPRING: Mating season extends from December through June, followed by a sixty-five-day gestation. Litter size averages three pups.

PREY/DIET: The maned wolf hunts small rodents and birds and has been known to prey on domestic chickens; it will also eat fruits and vegetable matter.

STATUS: The maned wolf is presumed highly endangered or extinct in Bolivia and Uruguay, though its populations may be increasing somewhat in Argentina and Brazil.

TASMANIAN WOLF

Thylacinus cynocephalus

Also called thylacine or Tasmanian tiger

Not a wolf or even a canine, the Tasmanian wolf is a marsupial carnivore, whose evolution was convergent with placental canines, particularly wolves.

DISTRIBUTION: The woodlands and open grasslands of Tasmania are home to the Tasmanian wolf. Its prehistoric range included New Guinea, mainland Australia, and Tasmania, but introduction of the dingo caused extinction in New Guinea and on the Australian mainland. Only in Tasmania, where dingoes were never introduced, did the Tasmanian wolf survive.

DESCRIPTION: The largest carnivorous marsupial, the Tasmanian wolf stands two feet high (61cm) at the shoulder and reaches more than six feet (1.8m) in length. It is wolflike in appearance. The fawn-colored to grayish brown coat has distinctive "tiger-stripe" markings along the back.

SOCIABILITY: Though often solitary, the Tasmanian wolf has been reported to have hunted in pairs or small groups (these may be young following their mothers to learn hunting skills).

OFFSPRING: Litters are from one to four young; like all marsupials, offspring are poorly developed at birth and remain in the pouch for about three months, until the female caches them in a rock shelter or secluded spot.

PREY/DIET: The Tasmanian wolf hunts birds, kangaroos, wallabies, and other mammals. The ability to open its jaws wider than any other mammal (as wide as 120 degrees) increases the penetration of its bite.

STATUS: Tasmanian wolves are listed as critically endangered, though none has been seen in more than fifty years. The last Tasmanian wolf in captivity died in 1936. A sanctuary still exists in the hope that a few of these animals have somehow survived in remote areas.

COYOTE

Canis latrans

Also called prairie wolf or brush wolf

The word *coyote* comes from the Aztec word *coyotl*, which means "barking dog." Some Native American tribes called the coyote "little wolf."

DISTRIBUTION: Historically, the coyote ranged the Great Plains and western United States; it now occurs throughout the continental United States and south central Canada, and ranges as far south as Mexico and northern areas of Central America.

DESCRIPTION: Generally one-third to one-half the size of wolves, coyotes average twenty inches (51cm) high at the shoulder and weigh about thirty-five pounds (16kg), though there is considerable variation depending on habitat. The coyote's tawny to rusty brown coat is peppered with dark gray, brown, and black. Black markings also occur around the eyes and on the tail, with the tip of the tail a solid black. Fur on underparts is generally lighter.

SOCIABILITY: Coyotes usually live in pairs but adopt cooperative hunting habits as needed.

OFFSPRING: Coyotes breed in January and February, with a gestation of sixty to sixty-five days; the average litter size is six, but may be higher. Offspring disperse between the first autumn and the end of the first year.

PREY/DIET: Coyotes prey on birds, hares, rabbits, rodents, and squirrels; they will also eat some fruits and insects.

STATUS: Unlike most of its canine relatives, the coyote's range is expanding because it has adapted to life close to humans. This is remarkable, because humans have long tried to destroy coyotes with poisons, traps, and guns. Reduced competition from declining gray wolf populations may have given coyotes greater opportunities for survival.

JACKALS

Jackal species include the side-striped jackal (Canis adustus), *the golden jackal* (Canis aureus), *and the black-backed jackal or silver-backed jackal* (Canis mesomelas)

DISTRIBUTION: Jackals range Africa and the Middle East. In some areas of Africa, all three jackal species can maintain sizable populations.

DESCRIPTION: Males average twenty-one pounds (9.5kg); females are slightly smaller. The side-striped jackal carries a stripe of pale guard hairs on the side of its grayish coat. The golden jackal varies from gold to grayish yellow with a reddish caste. The black-backed jackal's creamy to reddish coat is broken up by its distinctive black and silver pattern from the shoulder to the tip of the tail.

SOCIABILITY: Jackals live mostly in pairs and in family groups after breeding.

OFFSPRING: Gestation is fifty-seven to seventy days (sixty-three for the golden jackal) with an average litter size of three to four pups. Offspring disperse at about one year (slightly earlier for black-backed jackals).

PREY/DIET: The side-striped jackal is omnivorous, subsisting on a diet of vegetation, rodents, and invertebrates. The golden jackal preys on rodents, insects, young gazelles, birds, and fruit. The black-backed jackal is an opportunistic feeder, often scavenging from lions or hyenas after a kill.

STATUS: The side-striped jackal is generally considered rare. The golden jackal's populations are relatively stable. The black-backed jackal suffers much pressure from the destruction of lion populations and of prey species. It is also trapped for its fur and killed after conflicts with farmers.

DOMESTIC DOG

Canis familiaris

DISTRIBUTION: The domestic dog is found worldwide.

DESCRIPTION: With the greatest variation in size of any canid, the domestic dog ranges from tiny Chihuahuas to imposing mastiffs. The domestic dog boasts the greatest variation in coloration of any mammal, with coats ranging from pure white to darkest black.

SOCIABILITY: Domestic dogs, in general, are highly sociable.

OFFSPRING: Breeding takes place twice a year with a sixty-three-day gestation period.

PREY/DIET: The domestic dog is dependent on humans for food.

STATUS: Due to its popularity with humans, overpopulation and inbreeding have become the domestic dog's most serious problems.

DINGO

Canis familiaris dingo

DISTRIBUTION: Dingoes are probably descended from domestic dogs introduced to Australia by man about eight thousand years ago.

DESCRIPTION: Great variation in size exists among dingoes, who range from fifteen to twenty-five inches (38 to 63.5cm) high at the shoulder and weigh forty-eight pounds (22kg) or more. The dingoes has a pale to reddish cinnamon coat with variable white markings on the chest, feet, or tail.

SOCIABILITY: Dingoes live in family groups or small packs.

OFFSPRING: Dingoes breed only once a year, in March or April. Gestation is sixty-three days, with the litter containing up to ten pups, though the average is five to six.

PREY/DIET: Dingoes hunt mainly kangaroos and wallabies, as well as rabbits.

STATUS: Bounties are still paid for slain dingoes, as they are seen as sheep killers. In recent years extensive crossbreeding between dingoes and domestic dogs has begun to blur the line between the two.

RED FOX

Vulpes vulpes

DISTRIBUTION: Now the most widely distributed canid in the world, the red fox's huge range corresponds closely to the former range of the gray wolf. The red fox ranges throughout most of North America, Europe, and northern and central asia. It was also introduced to Australia and some of the Pacific Islands in the nineteenth century.

DESCRIPTION: The largest member of the genus *Vulpes*, the red fox's size varies, with males larger than females.

Animals living in northern areas are the largest and may weigh as much as thirty pounds (13.5kg), though they average about twenty-two pounds (10kg). While many members of this species do exhibit the rufous, or reddish, coat for which the red fox is named, the coat colors actually vary significantly and range from pale yellow to black.

SOCIABILITY: Mated pairs are sometimes accompanied by offspring. The red fox is highly territorial.

OFFSPRING: Mating occurs between December and April, and gestation is about fifty-two days. The average litter of three to four cubs matures at about ten months.

PREY/DIET: Red foxes subsist on a diet of rodents and other small animals, along with vegetables and fruits. Its keen sense of hearing helps make it an efficient hunter.

STATUS: Due to its adaptability and cunning, the species is thriving, even while it faces great pressures from hunting and diseases.

ARCTIC FOX

Alopex lagopus

DISTRIBUTION: Circumpolar distribution, ranging from northern polar regions through tundra regions of Alaska, Canada, and coastal Eurasia. The only canid that has successfully adapted to life in the far north.

DESCRIPTION: Males average seven to eight pounds (3 to 3.5kg) and are heavier than females. Arctic foxes have small ears, short legs, and bushy tails up to twelve inches long (30.5cm). Their fur may be blue-gray (the dominant form) or white. Both color forms go through seasonal changes, with the pale blue or silver-gray winter coat turning a dark brown in the spring and the bright white winter coat turning a pale brownish gray.

SOCIABILITY: Arctic foxes live mostly in pairs. The males assist with the rearing of offspring, and in some

areas, female offspring from the previous year act as "mother's helpers" for the first two months after birth.

OFFSPRING: Litter size corresponds to the availability of food (notably lemmings). Females give birth in underground dens after a fifty-two-day gestation period, and kits reach maturity at about ten months.

PREY/DIET: Rodents, particularly lemmings, are the arctic fox's main prey, and it will also scavenge from wolf kills. The arctic fox will also eat fish and some vegetation (especially when other food is scarce).

STATUS: Populations are relatively stable.

GRAY FOX

Urocyon cinereoargenteus

Also called the tree-climbing fox

DISTRIBUTION: The only wild canid whose current range includes both North and South America. this agile climber is not found in the Great Plains or desert, where it would be without its protective tree cover.

DESCRIPTION: The gray fox stands fourteen inches (35.5cm) tall at the shoulder. The gray fox sports coarse fur with silver-gray marking against a reddish gold background.

SOCIABILITY: Gray foxes generally live in pairs.

OFFSPRING: Dens may be kept in trees as high as thirty feet (9m) off the ground. Gestation lasts fifty-nine days, with litters averaging four cubs.

PREY/DIET: Small mammals, birds, and insects, as well as fruits and vegetables, are mainstays of the gray fox's diet.

STATUS: While the gray fox is not currently threatened, its population requires careful monitoring because of increasing demands for its fur; nearly half a million gray foxes are trapped each year for the fur market.

FENNEC

Fennecus zerda

DISTRIBUTION: The fennec inhabits the deserts of North Africa as well as the Sinai and Arabian peninsulas.

DESCRIPTION: The smallest of all the wild canids, the fennec stands eight inches (20.5cm) at the shoulder. Its large ears (six inches [15cm] long) help to control body heat. Its pale creamy to fawn fur reflects heat during the day and blends well with the fennec's sandy habitat. Hair on the soles of its feet provide protection from the burning sand of the African desert.

SOCIABILITY: Fennecs are relatively social; breeding pairs are surrounded by their offspring.

OFFSPRING: Litters consist of two to five kits, born after a forty-nine- to fifty-day gestation, that become mature at about one year.

PREY/DIET: Small rodents, roots, birds, insects, and eggs make up the bulk of the fennec's diet.

STATUS: The fennec is endangered throughout its range.

AFRICAN HUNTING DOG

Lycaon pictus

Also called the African wild dog or the Cape hunting dog

DISTRIBUTION: The African hunting dog lives primarily on the African savannas, though its range once covered nearly all of the African continent.

DESCRIPTION: The African hunting dog stands thirty inches (76cm) at the shoulder and averages fifty-five pounds (25kg). It has large, rounded ears and a short, broad muzzle; forefeet have four toes rather than five.

The only "spotted" wild dog, the African hunting dog's spots are actually highly individual blotchy markings of golden red, black, and white. Its bushy tail often carries a white tip.

SOCIABILITY: Extremely social and highly nomadic, the males and females maintain separate dominance hierarchies with females more aggressive than males. Packs number six to twenty members or more (historically, packs of hundreds of African hunting dogs lived and roamed together).

OFFSPRING: An average litter of seven to ten pups is born after a ten-week gestation period. The young are reared in dens burrowed in the ground. Male offspring often remain with their packs throughout their lives, while females disperse.

PREY/DIET: The African hunting dog preys on gazelles, impalas, zebras, and greater kudu (a type of wild cattle that can weigh 500 to 650 pounds [227 to 295kg]). Extremely fast, with keen eyesight, these effective hunters can pursue prey at up to thirty miles per hour (48kph) for great distances.

STATUS: Already extinct in much of its former range, its numbers are still decreasing.

BUSH DOG

Speothos venaticus

DISTRIBUTION: The bush dog ranges from Panama south through much of northern South America.

DESCRIPTION: Standing twelve inches (30.5cm) tall at the shoulder and reaching about twenty-five inches (63.5cm) in length, the bush dog has small ears and a short tail. Its coat is dark brown with darker fur on the underparts.

SOCIABILITY: Bush dogs live in hierarchical packs.

OFFSPRING: Litters average four to six pups. Females give birth in underground burrows or tree trunks after a gestation of two months.

PREY/DIET: Strong swimmers, bush dogs hunt water rodents such as agoutis and capybaras.

STATUS: Bush dogs are rare throughout their range and, in some areas, are in danger of extinction.

DHOLE

Cuon alpinus

Also called the Asiatic wild dog

DISTRIBUTION: The dhole's vast range extends through central and eastern Asia.

DESCRIPTION: Males, at forty pounds (18kg), are larger than females, which reach about twenty-five pounds (11.5kg). Height varies from fifteen to twenty inches (38 to 51cm) at the shoulder. Coloring ranges from grayish brown to golden red, with some black on the back and tail. White markings on the throat may continue to the chest.

SOCIABILITY: Dholes live in packs of five to a dozen related members. Sometimes two or more packs come together before the mating period to form clans of forty or more members, then split up when breeding season begins. All pack members help feed the pups.

OFFSPRING: Gestation is for sixty-three days. Females give birth in underground dens to litters of four to ten pups, which are mature at about one year.

PREY/DIET: Dholes hunt mainly deer, sheep, and rodents.

STATUS: Numerous in some parts of its range, the dhole is threatened in others.

Wolves, Dogs, And Hybrids

While some scientists feel that more than one type of wolf or a cross between wolves and jackals was responsible for the creation of man's best friend, most believe that the gray wolf is the true ancestor of the domestic dog.

Several significant differences (both anatomical and behavioral) between dogs and jackals point to the gray wolf as the likely forefather of the dog. Like wolves, dogs are pack animals, while jackals usually live in pairs. Wolves and domestic dogs are both highly social animals and have similar tooth and bone structures. While huskies, malamutes, and German shepherds most resemble the wolf, all of the more than 350 different breeds of domestic dogs, from the smallest Chihuahua to the most massive Saint Bernard, claim the gray wolf as their ancestor.

It is vital that we recognize the important differences between wolves and domestic dogs. Most importantly, we must understand fully that while our domestic companions have been conditioned to live among people, wild wolves do not share this characteristic. Wolves belong with other wolves!

Over a period of ten thousand to fifteen thousand years, humans have experimented with and selectively shaped the characteristics of the wolf, creating domestic dogs that are tractable and trainable as well as extremely varied in terms of physical characteristics. No other domestic animal exhibits such a vast range of colors, coats, sizes, and behaviors as the dog; indeed, some pedigreed dog breeds bear almost no resemblance to the wolves they claim as their wild ancestors. In fact, many of the characteristics that make certain dog breeds popular—whether short legs, flat faces, or miniature sizes—would only hinder or make impossible the survival of these animals in the wild. These domestic dogs were fashioned to fit human needs rather than the requirements of nature.

In recent years, a new and unfortunate breed has become popular in the United States—the wolf-dog hybrid. Wolf-dog hybrids now abound, with estimates in excess of 600,000 in the United States alone. That number will undoubtedly increase substantially in the next few years with estimates of as many as 150,000 new hybrid pups available on the market each year.

After working for thousands of years to transform the predator that is the wolf into a domestic companion that happily and peacefully accepts life in a confined area, surrounded by other small animals and children, we are stepping backward. The animals created from these hybrid unions cannot live safely in our human world or in the wild—they are neither wolf nor dog. The results can prove tragic for the animals them-

ABOVE: Wolf-dog hybrids appeal to dog owners because of their large size and wild beauty, but this animal is ill-equipped to live among humans. Its unpredictable nature makes it a threat to children, other family pets, and even its owner, whom the wolf-dog hybrid may view as an animal to be challenged for dominance.

FAMILY TRAITS

There are some important similarities and differences between wolves and domestic dogs:

■ Even German shepherds and huskies, though quite similar to wolves, do not have legs as long, chests as narrow, or feet as big proportionally as their wild ancestor.

■ As they walk, wolves swing their hind legs in the same line as their front legs. Domestic dogs, on the other hand, swing their hind legs between the tracks of their forelegs.

■ The wolf's muzzle is longer than those of most domestic breeds (the collie's comes closest in size to the wolf's). The wolf's incredibly powerful jaws are capable of exerting about fifteen hundred pounds (681kg) of pressure per square inch—about twice the pressure a strong domestic dog is capable of producing.

■ Wolves generally carry their tails hanging down, while many domestic dogs curl their tails over their backs.

■ Domestic dogs have lost the specialized scent gland found at the base of the wolf's tail, but domestic dogs, like wolves, use urine marking to scent their territories.

■ The gestation period for both wolves and domestic dogs is about sixty-three days, though domestic dogs can breed twice a year while wolves have a single breeding season per year.

■ Wolves and dogs can mate with each other and produce fertile offspring, though this rarely occurs in natural situations.

■ Many domestic dogs, like wolves, will gorge their food, a habit that has become known as "wolfing."

■ Communication patterns such as tucking their tails between their legs when frightened, bristling their fur to look larger and more intimidating when challenged, and snarling with lips curled up to display their impressive canines when angry are traits shared by wolves and domestic dogs.

■ Wolves and domestic dogs share some of the same enemies in the form of parasites and diseases. In fact, the spread of canine diseases from contact with domestic dogs is one of the major threats to surviving and recovering populations of wolves and other wild canids.

selves, for the person who may be injured by them, and for the few wolves living in the wild (where many wolf-dog hybrids are dumped by frustrated owners) who are at risk from the diseases these hybrids can carry.

These wolf-dog hybrids are often quite large, reaching weights of 150 pounds (68kg) or more. They may share the wolf's high intelligence and need for constant socializing; finding a life of relative confinement frustrating and unacceptable, they often become destructive or seek escape.

Wolf-dog hybrids may also retain the predatory nature of the wolf and, without the opportunities to pursue natural prey, have been known to kill livestock, pets, and children. Wolves show great control over aggression, while many domestic dogs have been bred by humans specifically for guarding territories and fighting. Most wolf-dog hybrids are not aggressive by nature, but when placed in confined areas or in situations where they feel trapped or threatened, they can lash out unexpectedly.

Wolf-dog hybrids can be quite temperamental and are easily upset. Quite frequently, as they reach sexual maturity, they will challenge humans for dominance. When hybrids become unmanageable, some frustrated owners make the mistake of dumping them in the wild.

Ill-equipped to survive in the wild and lacking in hunting skills, many wolf-dog hybrids starve to death. Others attack livestock in their attempts to survive, and often wild wolves are blamed. The diseases these hybrids may carry can pose devastating threats for wolves. Parvovirus and canine distemper heartworm, for instance, can be lethal to wild populations.

Laws regarding wolf-dog hybrids vary from state to state and among various county or municipal jurisdictions in the United States. Some forbid wolf-dog hybrids entirely; others regulate them as wild or exotic animals. In some areas, wolf-dog hybrids are subject to the same laws that apply to domestic dogs or to dangerous dogs. That so much attention is now focused on the dangers of wolf-dog hybrids is no idle concern. The most important constant among these wolf-dog hybrids is their unpredictability.

What's In a Name?

The classification, or taxonomy, of plants and animals is not a static science. Originally, distinctions between species or subspecies were based mainly on physical traits (such as skull size and features, variations in coat patterns and characteristics, and relative size) or on differences in geographic distribution.

Taxonomy is in an almost constant state of flux—particularly as new techniques in genetics allow scientists to get a clearer view of basic similarities and differences between animals.

Opinion varies as to the number of different wolf species and subspecies. In North America alone, as many as twenty-four subspecies of *Canis lupus* were once recognized. Today, scientists believe *Canis lupus* is more accurately represented by only five or six subspecies.

Let's take a look at how the eastern timber wolf, for instance, is classified:

Kingdom	Animalia
Phylum	Chordata
Subphylum	Vertebrata
Class	Mammalia
Order	Carnivora
Family	Canidae
Genus	*Canis*
Species	*lupus*
Subspecies	*lycaon*

Canis lupus, the gray wolf, is a mammal, a carnivore, a canine, and a wolf. The subspecific name *lycaon* refers to a character in Greek mythology; Lycaon, king of Arcadia, was turned into a wolf by Zeus as a punishment. The common name is, perhaps, more descriptive in that the range of the eastern timber wolf included the eastern forested areas of North America.

Some of the many descriptive subspecific names once or still recognized for the gray wolf follow.

ALCES Referring to this wolf's dependence on very large moose, which are themselves classified as *Alces alces*. The Kenai Peninsula wolf, *Canis lupus alces*.

BAILEYI Named after a government trapper. The Mexican wolf, *Canis lupus baileyi*.

CAMPESTRIS "The wolf of the open plains." The steppe wolf, *Canis lupus campestris*.

COLUMBIANUS The British Columbia wolf, *Canis lupus columbianus*.

FUSCUS "Tawny," referring to the coat color of the Cascade Mountains wolf, *Canis lupus fuscus*.

HUDSONICUS The Hudson Bay wolf, *Canis lupus hudsonicus*, ranged west and north of Hudson Bay.

LABRADORIUS The Labrador wolf, *Canis lupus labradorius*, had a distribution throughout northern Quebec and Labrador.

NUBILUS "Cloudy" or "cloudy gray," referring to the generally pale gray coloration of animals that once roamed the Great Plains. The Buffalo wolf, *Canis lupus nubilus*.

OCCIDENTALIS The "western" wolf, also known as the Mackenzie Valley wolf, *Canis lupus occidentalis*.

ORION Another reference to mythology, comparing the wolf to the great hunter Orion. The Greenland wolf, *Canis lupus orion*.

YOUNGI Refers to a government hunter who helped spread wolf tales and lore in the 1940s and 1950s. The southern Rocky Mountain wolf, *Canis lupus youngi*.

Carnivores, Herbivores, And Omnivores

Simple, right? Well, not exactly. It's not that all carnivores never eat plants, but that their diets consist mainly of animal matter. And some herbivores will supplement their main diet of plants with meat. Animals whose diets include a variety of animal and plant foods are known as omnivores.

While most members of the taxonomic order Carnivora also fall within the dietary category of carnivores, this is not absolute. The giant panda takes its place among the Carnivora with the bears, though its diet—made up mainly of bamboo—definitely categorizes the giant panda as a herbivore.

Most true meat eaters that depend on other animals as prey have smaller populations than do herbivores. This is because these predators are higher up on the food chain, and food becomes more scarce at the top.

Because this scarce supply of food is also quick, mobile, and adept at defending itself with powerful kicks or other mechanisms, carnivores must be alert, intelligent, and strong to catch their dinner and thus survive. Herbivores don't experience these same feeding problems.

ABOVE: Wolves are carnivores that depend on hunting herbivores such as this white-tailed deer for their survival. Availability of this prey is not always certain, so wolves have adapted to a feast-and-famine existence. When they are successful in the hunt, they will make the most of their meal, eating as much as twenty pounds (9kg) each, then perhaps eating nothing for several days. **OVERLEAF:** Even a fleeting glimpse of a wolf in the wild is nothing short of awe-inspiring.

Chapter 3

Wolves Around the World

IN WILDERNESS

IS THE PRESERVATION

OF THE WORLD.

—HENRY DAVID THOREAU

Timber to Tundra and Peaks to Plains

Once the most wide-ranging land mammal in the world, the wolf *Canis lupus* was one of the most successful hunters ever to walk the earth because of its exceptional ability to survive in such a wide variety of climates and habitats. Indeed, the wolf could once be found throughout the Northern Hemisphere, wherever there were suitable species on which to prey and thereby survive.

While their numbers have plummeted after years of persecution, wolves still live in a wide variety of habitats, from the deserts to the frozen far north and from the grasslands to the forests. Their remaining populations do tend, whenever possible, to live in areas away from established human settlements.

Both wolves and humans adopted the lifestyle of plains-dwelling, collective hunters, but in the competition for the large, plains-dwelling prey species, the wolf ultimately lost out to man and his technology.

Life on the plains usually means life in a group. Among the wide-open spaces, there is safety in numbers if you're a herbivore and strength in numbers if you're a carnivore. Speed, strength, endurance, and sociability are characteristics that serve the wolf well in a plains habitat. Their high intelligence allows wolves to coordinate their efforts to cull a young or weak animal from the herd, isolating it from its counterparts.

This primary adaptation of cooperative hunting is vital for an animal whose survival depends on bringing down prey many times its size, such as large elk, caribou, deer, and, in some parts of the wolf's range, musk oxen, moose, or bison, which may tip the scales at more than a thousand pounds (454kg).

While the wolf is superbly adapted to life on the plains, its survival has been greatly enhanced by its flexibility and adaptation to a variety of habitats. Pressures from human encroachment on the plains have pushed the wolf and many other species, including the grizzly bear *(Ursus arctos)* and the wapiti *(Cervus elaphus)*, into mountainous areas less hospitable to humans.

In mountainous regions, winds increase, temperatures drop, and more rain falls. Wolves who live in the high mountains or the far north, where there is snow on the ground most of the year, have stockier bodies and shorter ears, tails, and limbs to increase their tolerance of the cold. Fur that is longer and coarser than that of its plains counterparts and a dense undercoat also help wolves in norther climates conserve body heat. The arctic wolf, for example, grows long, thick, white fur on its legs and between the pads on its feet during the winter months as protection from the intense cold. Other wolves face the extreme heat and aridity of the desert. If wolves in colder

ABOVE AND OPPOSITE: While wolves don't need an absolutely pristine and unpeopled wilderness in order to survive, the severe pressures of encroaching human populations have rendered much of the continental United States uninhabitable by wolves. Protected conservation areas and national parks represent our biggest hope of preserving the type of wilderness needed to sustain viable wolf populations.

climates are larger and stockier, it is no surprise that desert subspecies are smaller than either their timber or tundra relatives. In the deserts of Israel, variations in body size seem to correspond to fluctuations in annual rainfall levels. The larger, darker members of the subspecies *Canis lupus pallipes* live predominantly in the northwestern Negev, where rainfall levels are relatively high. In the southern Negev, where rain is scarcer, lives the smaller and more lightly colored *Canis lupus arabs*.

Scientists have only recently recognized that the earth's most critically endangered canid is a wolf. This beautiful canid, with its bright reddish coat and distinctive white markings on the chest, neck, and throat, was formerly considered a jackal. Recent genetic research, studies of pack structure that show a strong social hierarchy, and other behavioral similarities to the northern gray wolf have led to the belief that *Canis simensis* should be classified as a wolf rather than a jackal. There are fewer than five hundred Ethiopian wolves in the wild, who face loss of habitat, persecution, and an influx of diseases as domestic dogs join the people moving into the region. Without drastic measures to preserve this species, however, extinction may be imminent in the next few years.

After centuries of persecution and habitat destruction, wolves around the world are forced further and further from human settlements or are forced to depend on human intervention and protection for survival. Much of the gray wolf's former range in Europe and North America is now occupied by the red fox and the coyote, respectively.

The future will tell if there is room in the world for two such highly sociable and intelligent predators as humans and wolves.

ABOVE: Wolves historically have lived in an array of habitats, but much of their current range is in the north. There, the human population is less dense, and thus wolves face fewer threats from human settlements.

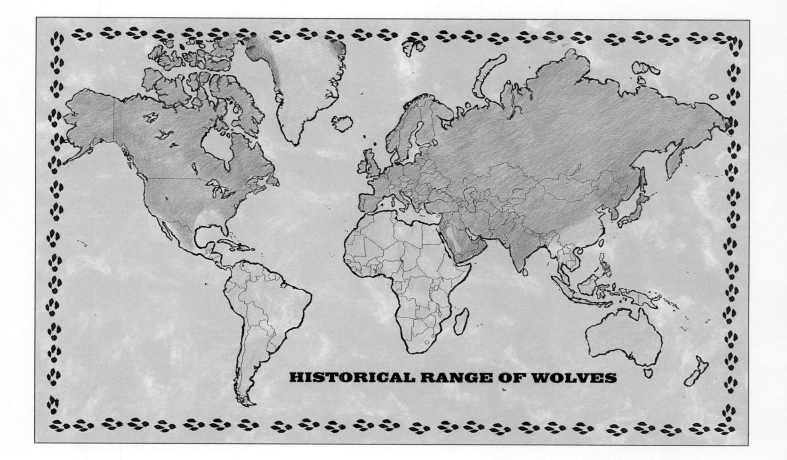

HISTORICAL RANGE OF WOLVES

WORLDWIDE WOLF WATCH

NORTH AMERICA

There are perhaps nine thousand to ten thousand wolves in the United States and fifty thousand to sixty thousand in Canada; it is questionable whether any still exist in Mexico. In the United States, the largest population of wolves is in Alaska. Throughout the lower forty-eight states, with the exception of Minnesota, the wolf is classified as endangered. Minnesota is home to between twelve hundred and two thousand wolves. There, they are classified as threatened. Canada's wolf population is stable, and is even increasing in some areas. In certain regions, wolves are protected; in others, they are hunted and trapped as big game and fur bearers.

UNITED STATES

ALASKA

Population Estimate: 5,000 to 8,000

Status Report: Wolves are hunted and trapped in season as big game and fur bearers and through government-sponsored management programs

Prey Species: Moose, caribou, sheep, deer, beaver, goat

IDAHO

Population Estimate: 15

Status Report: Endangered

Prey Species: Deer, elk

MICHIGAN

Population Estimate: 57 on Upper Peninsula Mainland; 17 on Isle Royale National Park

Status Report: Endangered, but increasing
populations

Prey Species: Moose, white-tailed deer, beaver,
snowshoe hare

MINNESOTA

Population Estimate: 1,200 to 2,000

Status Report: Threatened; protected species

Prey Species: White-tailed deer, moose, beaver,
snowshoe hare

MONTANA

Population Estimate: 65

Status Report: Endangered, but increasing populations

Prey Species: Deer, elk

NORTH CAROLINA

Population Estimate: 50 (red wolves)

Status Report: Experimental nonessential reintroduction status

Prey Species: White-tailed deer, raccoon,
nutria

TENNESSEE

Population Estimate: 6 (red wolves)

Status Report: Experimental nonessential reintroduction status in Great Smoky
Mountains National Park

Prey Species: White-tailed deer, raccoon

WASHINGTON

Population Estimate: Uncertain; possible 5 or fewer

Status Report: Endangered

Prey Species: Deer, elk

WISCONSIN

Population Estimate: 50 to 57

Status Report: Endangered, but
increasing population

Prey Species: Deer, beaver, and snowshoe hare

WYOMING

Population Estimate: 14 reintroduced into Yellowstone
National Park

Status Report: Endangered, experimental
nonessential reintroduction status

Prey Species: Deer, elk

CANADA

ALBERTA

Population Estimate: 4,000 to 5,000

Status Report: Classified as fur bearer—hunted
and trapped

Prey Species: Moose, caribou, sheep, deer,
beaver, goat, elk, bison

BRITISH COLUMBIA, YUKON TERRITORY

Population Estimate: 8,000 to 10,000

Status Report: Classified as game species and
fur bearer—hunted and trapped

Prey Species: Moose, caribou, sheep, beaver

NORTHWEST TERRITORIES

Population Estimate: 5,000 to 15,000

Status Report: Classified as fur bearer—hunted
and trapped

Prey Species: Moose, caribou, sheep, deer,
beaver, goat

ONTARIO/QUEBEC

Population Estimate: 10,000 to 12,000

Status Report: Classified as fur bearer—hunted
and trapped

Prey Species: Moose, deer, caribou, beaver

GREENLAND

Population Estimate: 50 to 100

Status Report: Threatened; protected year-
round throughout most of its
range

Prey Species: Musk-oxen, caribou

MEXICO

Population Estimate: Uncertain; possibly extinct; if
small population exists, likely
less than 10 animals as lone
wolves and/or pairs

Status Report: Granted full protection but
unenforced—population decline
because of persecution and habitat
destruction; draft Environmental
Impact Statement provided for
public review and comment on
potential reintroduction plan to
proposed sites in the United States

Prey Species: Mostly livestock

EUROPE

Once, large wolf populations roamed throughout most of Europe. Today, only remnants of those populations remain, and in some areas, the wolf is long gone. In addition to the war against wolves, recent wars between humans in Europe have had a negative effect on the remaining wolf populations. Wolves are beginning to immigrate from the former Soviet Union into some areas, such as Finland. In

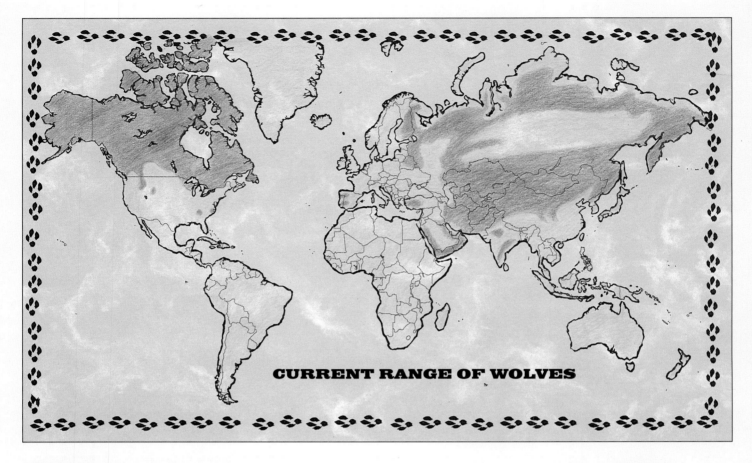

CURRENT RANGE OF WOLVES

1993 a new law was passed allowing the hunting of wolves in northern regions. Wolves are also migrating into France from Italy, and into Poland from the former Soviet Union.

In many areas of Europe very little wild prey remains on which predators like wolves can survive. The largest populations of wolves are often found in rugged mountainous areas where larger populations of native prey provide an ample food supply.

BOSNIA/HERZEGOVINA

Population Estimate: 400
Status Report: Unprotected; wolf populations declining because of the effects of war within the former Yugoslavia
Prey Species: Mouflon, roe deer, red deer

BULGARIA

Population Estimate: About 100 wolves, mostly lone wolves
Status Report: Highly threatened with no protection, populations declining because of persecution and habitat destruction
Prey Species: Moose, roe deer, red deer, wild boar, mouflon

CROATIA

Population Estimate: 30 to 50
Status Report: Removed from list of game species in 1994; a Croatian wolf group was formed to lobby for wolf protection and to provide public education about wolves

Prey Species: Roe deer, dogs, sheep

FINLAND

Population Estimate: Fewer than 100
Status Report: Endangered; protected in the south, but no protection in the north where hunting is allowed from November through March in reindeer herding areas; in the east they are classified as game
Prey Species: Moose, reindeer, white-tailed deer, livestock

FRANCE

Population Estimate: 7 to 15
Status Report: Wolves recently migrated into France from Italy after a long absence, and have received full protection with the stipulation that the government can kill any wolves determined to be dangerous.
Prey Species: Roe deer, chamois, mouflon

GERMANY

Population Estimate: Fewer than 10 but increasing with wolf immigration via Poland
Status Report: Protected
Prey Species: Red deer, roe deer, wild boar

GREECE

Population Estimate: 500 in northern Greece

Status Report: Extinct in southern Greece since the 1930s; partial protection only in northern Greece, with active hunting and poisoning; population decline because of persecution, habitat destruction, and decline of wild prey populations

Prey Species: Deer, wild boar, chamois, livestock

HUNGARY

Population Estimate: Uncertain; probably fewer than 50

Status Report: Two small breeding populations of wolves were recently identified in Hungary after an absence of many decades—one is in the northeast near the Ukraine border; the second is in south central Hungary

Prey Species: Roe deer, red deer

ITALY

Population Estimate: Uncertain; estimates vary from 250 to 450

Status Report: Highly threatened and receiving protection; population now centered in the southern and central Apennines

Prey Species: Deer, wild boar, livestock, garbage, mouflon

NORWAY/SWEDEN

Population Estimate: Norway: a few lone wolves; Sweden: 17, mostly lone wolves and pairs

Status Report: Highly endangered; full protection granted, but negative public attitudes still surround the wolf

Prey Species: Moose, reindeer, livestock

POLAND

Population Estimate: 850 to 900; wolves have been immigrating into Poland from the former Soviet Union

Status Report: Classified as game species with partial protection from April through October

Prey Species: Red deer, wild boar, roe deer, moose, mouflon

PORTUGAL

Population Estimate: 150 to 300

Status Report: Fully protected since 1988, though illegal hunting and poaching are common

Prey Species: Domestic goats, sheep, horses

ROMANIA

Population Estimate: 2,000 to 2,500

Status Report: No protection; hunted and trapped, bounty paid for wolf skins; greatest protection comes from the rugged character of the Carpathian Mountains that are home to these wolves

Prey Species: Red deer, roe deer, wild boar, sheep, dogs

SLOVAKIA

Population Estimate: Uncertain, possibly around 300—mostly in the mountainous areas near the Polish border

Status Report: Partial protection—still hunted

Prey Species: Red deer, wild boar, roe deer

SLOVENIA

Population Estimate: 15 to 20

Status Report: Protected; wolf populations declined because of the effects of war within the former Yugoslavia

Prey Species: Mouflon, roe deer, red deer

SPAIN

Population Estimate: Uncertain; estimates vary widely from 150 to 1,000

Status Report: Partial protection but highly threatened by persecution and habitat destruction

Prey Species: Livestock, roe deer, wild boar

ASIA/EURASIA

The statistics from Europe clearly show that wolves are immigrating into many areas from the former Soviet Union, where one of the largest populations of wolves in the world exists today. Political turmoil has played havoc with efforts to preserve wolves and other species. Today, fifty thousand to ninety thousand wolves live in this vast area, though they are threatened. Persecution and habitat destruction have hit the wolf hard in the former Soviet Union—population numbers dropped to a low of twenty-five thousand to thirty thousand in the late 1980s. Wolf bounties were halted in 1990, though poaching is still a problem, particularly in the eastern areas, where pelts are easily transported into China and sold. The war on wolves has long been a heated one in China. Habitat loss is a major factor, but so are bounty programs, poisoning, and trapping. Today, no wolves exist in Hunan, Taiwan, or the southern regions of the country. Among other Asian areas, Iran has a strong wolf population. Three subspecies of wolves—*Canis lupus lupus*, *Canis lupus pallipes*, and *Canis lupus arabs*—are found in Israel, where full legal protection has been conferred upon the wolf.

CHINA
Population Estimate: Uncertain; possibly 400
Status Report: The wolf is unprotected in China and extermination efforts are ongoing; their numbers continue to decline because of extreme persecution and habitat destruction
Prey Species: Reeve's muntjac, wild boar, hare, Chinese water deer, saiga, livestock

INDIA
Population Estimate: 1,000 to 2,000
Status Report: Highly threatened from habitat destruction, lack of wild prey, and other effects from a burgeoning human population
Prey Species: Garbage; carrion

IRAN
Population Estimate: Greater than 1,000
Status Report: Classified as a game species and threatened by persecution
Prey Species: Gazelle, mountain sheep, livestock, wild boar, deer

ISRAEL
Population Estimate: 100 to 150
Status Report: Highly threatened from habitat destruction in particular; the wolf has received full legal protection since 1954
Prey Species: Gazelle, hare, garbage, carcasses of domestic animals

JORDAN
Population Estimate: 200
Status Report: Highly threatened; the wolf receives no protection and is declining because of persecution

Prey Species: Main prey unknown

LEBANON
Population Estimate: 10 or more as lone wolves or in pairs
Status Report: Highly endangered without any protection and facing continued persecution
Prey Species: Garbage, carrion

MONGOLIA
Population Estimate: 20,000 to 30,000
Status Report: No protection afforded; the wolf faces active extermination efforts and is the only animal in Mongolia that may be hunted all year long.
Prey Species: Saiga, wild game, domestic animals

SAUDI ARABIA
Population Estimate: 600 to 700
Status Report: Stable population
Prey Species: Sheep, goats, chickens, garbage

SYRIA
Population Estimate: 200 to 500
Status Report: Highly threatened and persecuted; no protection
Prey Species: Livestock, carrion

AFRICA
In the two areas of Africa where wolves remain, they are highly endangered. In fact, the Ethiopian wolf *Canis simensis* is considered the most critically endangered canid in the world.

EGYPT
Population Estimate: 30
Status Report: Highly endangered; the wolf receives no protection and faces heavy persecution
Prey Species: Hares, livestock

ETHIOPIA
Population Estimate: 500
Status Report: In danger of extinction, the wolf is protected by law in Ethiopia
Prey Species: Rodents, particularly giant mole rats

Life in the Wild—A Dangerous Livelihood

A POINT OF GREAT SIGNIFICANCE...IS THE KEEN SENSITIVITY OF THE

WOLF TO THE CONDITION OF ITS PREY. IN JUDGING WHAT HE CAN

HANDLE AND WHAT SHOULD PRUDENTLY BE LEFT ALONE, THIS CARNIVORE

BRINGS TO HIS DAILY WORK SOPHISTICATED SKILLS COMPLETELY BEYOND

OUR HUMAN KEN. THESE ARE MADE POSSIBLE BY INBORN CAPACITIES

EFFECTIVELY TUNED AND DEVELOPED IN THE YOUNG ANIMAL THROUGH

AN APPRENTICESHIP THAT ONLY THE CAPABLE SURVIVE.

—DURWARD L. ALLEN

Going the Distance

Hunger is a powerful driving force. To survive, wolves must eat. To survive throughout the year—particularly in those areas that for months may be covered in deep snow or ice—wolves must make excellent use of sharply honed skills, keen senses and intelligence, adaptable natures, and well-developed bodies. The wolf is superbly built for endurance.

Well muscled and powerful, mature wolves stand between twenty-six and thirty-three inches (66 and 84cm) at the shoulder. Adult male wolves weigh an average of seventy-five to a hundred pounds (34 to 45.5kg) and measure an impressive five to six and a half feet (1.5 to 2m) from nose to tip of tail. Females tend to be a bit smaller, though they are also quite powerful. Adult females average sixty to eighty-five pounds (27 to 38.5kg) and reach four and a half to six feet (1.3 to 1.8m) in length. The wolf's expressive tail may easily grow thirteen to twenty inches (33 to 51cm) long.

The wolf's incredible body strength and agility allow it to travel many miles over uneven terrain, through forests, plains, snow, and water in all kinds of weather.

There is truth to the old Russian proverb "The wolf is kept fed by its feet." Those feet leave an impressive mark. Front feet are larger than hind feet, and the tracks of adult wolves can measure five inches (12.5cm) or more in width. These massive feet spread out when wolves walk or run, providing traction and support on wet ground or snow. Their claws, too, help them grip when running. These claws are not retractable like those of cats, and nearly constant contact with the ground keeps them blunt. Long, powerful legs and an uncommonly narrow chest for a canid allow the wolf to run efficiently and with remarkable grace.

Wolves—like dogs, cats, and other animals that depend on swift, silent movements—walk and run on their toes. This is known as digitigrade movement, as opposed to the plantigrade, or flat-footed, movement used by humans, many other primates, and bears.

By running on their toes, wolves are able to turn quickly, even at great speed, and can keep up a steady pace for long periods of time. Wolves spend eight to ten hours each day on the move, trotting and running. They

ABOVE: Wolves were built for running. They usually trot when on the move and can keep up a steady pace for hours. Sometimes they break into a loping run and, when in pursuit of prey, give chase in bursts of speed up to forty miles per hour (64.5kph). It is not uncommon for wolves to be on the move eight to ten hours a day, covering distances of 30 to 125 miles (48 to 201km). **OPPOSITE:** A disperser, such as this lone gray wolf, usually exhibits a dominant personality and chooses to strike out on its own, leaving the confines of the pack's social structure in search of a partner and a territory where it can form a new pack. Such wolves are often fitted with radio collars, which allow researchers to track the wolves' travels. A lone wolf leads a difficult existence, risking encounters with rival packs as it passes through their territories. In order to keep a low profile, lone wolves rarely howl or scent mark. Dispersers usually make new homes close to their original packs, but occasionally travel great distances.

spend a third of their lives and at least half of their waking hours on foot, covering great distances, usually at a steady pace of about five miles per hour (8kph) while trotting or loping. They can average twenty-five miles per hour (40kph) for an extended period of time and in strong pursuit may reach speeds of thirty-five to forty miles per hour (56.5 to 64.5kph) for short bursts.

During the warm summer months, wolves generally are on the move early in the evening and don't return to the den or rendezvous site (a meeting place where pups spend the day and adults regroup for communal hunting after a period of solitary hunting) until late at night or early the next morning. The pack uses the hottest part of the day to get some much-needed rest, since running in the heat is neither comfortable nor efficient.

Wolves and other canids have sweat glands between their toes, but not over their entire bodies. During warm weather, wolves pant with their mouths open— breathing in through the nose and out through the mouth. The evaporating moisture helps keep their bodies cool.

But it is the cold weather for which wolves are best adapted. Their bodies, for the most part, are designed to keep heat in rather than to shed it. Thick, insulating fur keeps them warm, while their long legs and broad feet let them move well through snow or over ice. In fact, wolves may seek out frozen waterways for their winter routes because they find travel over solid ice relatively easy.

If overland routes are covered in deep snow, wolves travel in single file. While the lead wolf plows through the snow to break trail, the other pack members conserve their strength and energy by literally following in his footsteps over the narrow pathway. Several members of the pack may take turns in the lead position, so that no single wolf has to bear too great a burden. When the wolf pack encounters suitable paths created by traveling caribou, deer, or moose, they may travel these packed routes for a distance in order to conserve energy.

With her back against the wind and her body curled so that she can bury her nose, muzzle, or face in her thickly furred tail, a wolf can sleep comfortably even at temperatures of -40°F (-40°C). Wolves can also conserve heat at extremely cold temperatures by reducing the blood flow near skin surfaces.

Food for Thought

Wolves are carnivores, and cannot survive without killing other animals for their food. This is not a bloodthirsty act of violence (a judgment only humans can make) but simply an act of survival. A wolf could no more choose to survive on fruits and vegetable matter than a deer could decide to survive on meat. The wolf is an apex predator, like humans, and is at the top of its food chain. Wolves evolved over hundreds of thousands of years to fit this specialized role in nature—to hunt, to catch, and, yes, to kill large hoofed animals, or ungulates. While this is not a heinous act, nor is it an altruistic one. The wolf has made no conscious decision to cull the weak in service to a stronger herd. This is the outcome, however, and it is an important element of a healthy, balanced ecosystem.

Highly evolved cooperative hunting skills are responsible for wolves' success in bringing down animals much larger than themselves. It is likely that wolves evolved this style of pack hunting because a specific ecological niche remained open to them. While few single predators were large enough to kill bison, caribou, deer, moose, and musk oxen, these herd animals presented an abundant food source for the predator that could combine the strengths of many individuals and so overpower the massive ungulate.

IT JUST MAKES SCENTS

Wolves may come upon prey by chance, but more likely, they will detect the scent of prey animals on the wind or will follow a scent trail on the ground. Wolves have a superior sense of smell, and when they flare their nostrils, they inhale scent-rich moisture from which they glean important information about their surroundings.

This type of hunting requires great concentration, commitment, keen intelligence, and a willingness to work within a strict and clearly defined social structure.

But even under relatively good conditions, hunting is difficult. Wolves are successful only one out of every ten attempts. Healthy caribou or deer can usually outpace wolves, while healthy moose can stand their ground and intimidate even a large wolf pack. Large ungulates have size as an advantage, and most also come equipped with sharp hooves and antlers for protection. Even the largest moose can wield these weapons with great agility.

ABOVE: Young wolves develop strength and skills while playing. These nine-week-old pups enjoy a simple game of tug-of-war with some bones. Games of skill and strength help wolf pups develop their muscles as well as their personalities and dominance roles in the pack. **OVERLEAF:** A successful hunt is key to wolves' survival. Wolves might detect prey by picking up direct scents if the prey is nearby, by tracking, or by chance encounter. But discovery alone does not ensure success. Most prey animals, in fact, have so many avenues of escape that they elude wolves more often than not. Fewer than 10 percent of a wolf pack's hunting attempts result in a successful kill and a meal.

Because hunting carries a relatively low chance of success, wolves search for easy targets. Would a wolf eat a robust animal in its prime? It would if it had the chance—but such a chance rarely, if ever, comes the wolf's way. When wolves sight a healthy animal, they must weigh the cost of expending such large amounts of energy to pursue an animal that is likely to get away or defend itself successfully. It doesn't really make sense to waste vital energy on prey that has such advantages.

Instead, it is the vulnerable animals—the crippled, the diseased, the injured, those with poor sight or hearing, and the oldest or youngest—on which the wolf survives. In eliminating these weaker animals, the wolf helps maintain strong, viable populations of large ungulates such as caribou, deer, elk, and moose. By culling animals that are old or sick, the healthier animals have a greater chance of survival because contagious diseases are less likely to spread and there is less stress on food supplies. Wolf predation on young animals helps control ungulate populations and also reduces the number of animals competing for food.

Before a wolf pack devotes great amounts of time and, more importantly, energy, to pursuing prey, it tests the animal it has selected. Wolves will force their potential quarry to run or stand ground in defense. Wolves assess their potential for success with remarkable speed. If the prey animal vigorously defends itself, the wolves think twice about continuing the attack. They are fully aware of the damage that an animal such as a twelve-hundred-pound (545kg) moose bull can inflict. To be gored by antlers or kicked with heavy hooves means severe injury or even death. If injury to the wolves is probable, they save their energy and move on.

If, however, an individual exhibits any sign of weakness or injury (a limp, an inattentive mother, open wounds, substantial hair loss, or, behaviorists suspect, many conditions that are recognizable to wolves but not to humans), it will become the focus of the pack's attention regardless of the other animals nearby. If the animal runs, the pack is likely to follow. Particularly on ice or in deep snow, wolves, with their large feet, maneuver better than their hoofed prey and have a distinct advantage. The snow will often support the wolf's weight distributed over its snowshoelike

OPPORTUNISTIC EATERS

Like most predators, wolves are opportunists and will scavenge carrion and even occasionally kill livestock, though these acts are infrequent as long as populations of its natural prey remain more or less constant. Wolves resort to killing sheep and cattle when severe weather conditions or human interference cause an imbalance or grave fluctuation in wild populations.

feet, but ungulates may break through the snow's crust in slow and treacherous movements. The wolves will try to separate their chosen prey from the herd, surrounding and pursuing a single animal until it falls.

But wolves will chase prey for only so long; if success does not come quickly, the pack will usually abandon the effort and look for easier quarry. It simply isn't practical to expend more energy on a long-distance pursuit than would be recouped from eating the prey. Knowing when to move swiftly and silently and when to move slowly and deliberately seems instinctual with wolves. Stealth is critical because if prey animals become aware—by either picking up their scent or seeing them—that wolves are approaching, the prey may flee before the pack has a chance to attack.

Because their prey is generally much larger and swifter than they are, wolves make great use of any advantages they can find. Moving in close before attacking, approaching prey from upwind, surprising prey, or encircling prey to cut off escape routes may provide the few valuable seconds that assure a successful kill and an important meal. To wear out their quarry, one wolf may sprint while others lay back, surging ahead to take over when the lead wolf tires. The pack will snap at the animal's legs, rear, and sides to weaken it further. Once shock and exhaustion set in, the kill is assured.

While pursuing such challenging quarry requires lots of energy, the payoff is equally great. Hunting small prey expends energy with little return and so is relatively rare.

PREY SPECIES

DEER

While there are some general similarities among members of the deer family, there are also a great many differences. Almost all male deer grow antlers, but among female deer, only the caribou is endowed with antlers. It doesn't seem unusual that most female deer don't grow antlers when the main purpose of these impressive ornaments is considered. While antlers can, indeed, be used as defensive weapons against attacking predators, their real purpose is for another kind of fight. Sparring males use their antlers while vying for the rights to mate with females during the breeding season.

When defending themselves from predators such as wolves, deer are more likely to depend on the sharp, hard edges of their front hooves. Or, if they are near water, deer will charge in. Excellent swimmers all, most deer can easily outpace wolves in deep water. But the same slender legs and sharp hooves that give deer an advantage for running on land make traversing ice and hard-crusted snow very treacherous. In these cases, wolves are likely to overcome their prey.

Size is the area where different members of the deer family show the greatest variation. A mature male white-tailed deer (*Odocoileus virginianus*) averages 250 to 300 pounds (113.5 to 136kg). Huge bucks have even been recorded at four hundred pounds (181.5kg). The black-tailed deer (*Odocoileus columbianus*) is only slightly smaller in size. All deer are keenly alert and possess excellent hearing. The mule deer (*Odocoileus hemionus*), for instance, with its long, broad ears, can pick up even the faint snap of a twig from five hundred feet (152.5m) away. And, when the breeze is blowing in its direction, the deer can detect a wolf's scent from as far as eight hundred yards (731.5km) away.

The large red deer, or wapiti (*Cervus elaphus*), of North America are often inappropriately called elk. The misnomer most likely came from European colonists who thought that because of its size, the wapiti resembled the European elk. In fact, the European elk is a different species altogether; in North America it is known as the moose. Largest of the North American red deer subspecies is the Roosevelt's, or Olympic, wapiti (*Cervus elaphus roosevelti*). Second in size among the deer family only to the moose, a mature bull stands five and a half feet (1.6m) high at the shoulder and can weigh seven hundred to a thousand pounds (318 to 454kg). Cows average about five hundred to six hundred pounds (227 to 272.5kg). The Asiatic wapiti are closely related to the various North American subspecies.

In the Old World, caribou are known as reindeer. Their best defenses are their speed (up to fifty miles per hour [80.5kph] for short distances) and their habit of migrating in large herds (up to a 100,000 animals together), which can be intimidating and can force wolves to work hard at separating weak or disabled animals from the herd.

MOOSE

The largest representative of the deer family, a mature bull moose (*Alces alces*) may weigh an impressive thirteen hundred to fifteen hundred pounds (590 to 681kg) and stand six to seven and a half feet (1.8 to 2.3m) tall at the shoulder. Its antlers alone weigh fifty to sixty pounds (23 to 27kg) and may rise ten feet (3m) above the ground. Cows weigh in at 800 to 850 pounds (363 to 386kg). A full-grown moose measures eight to ten feet (2.5 to 3m) long from tip of nose to tail, and with its long legs, the moose's belly stands thirty-six to forty inches (91.5 to 101.5cm) off the ground. With this impressive stature, it isn't odd that a mature moose has few natural predators.

Newborn calves are the most vulnerable because they can't run well or defend themselves, and so they never stray far from their mothers. Cows choose the most secluded areas possible in which to give birth. Islands are favored as they provide the greatest variety of escape routes. Moose are strong swimmers, reaching

71

Even adult moose can be handicapped in winter by deep, heavily crusted snow or ice-covered lakes. The snow's crust can rarely support the weight of a moose as it can a wolf's, and the moose's sharp-edged hooves have no traction on ice. Bull moose are also weakened and vulnerable in autumn, when their energy is depleted by the rut.

Starvation, not wolves, has proven one of the greatest threats to many moose populations today. In areas where predators such as the wolf have been killed off, moose populations can increase to such an extent that their own food sources are destroyed. When severe winters set in, great numbers of moose starve. Starvation in winter is the greatest threat to many species of deer.

HARES AND RABBITS

Hares and rabbits have little chance of fighting back against a wolf. Their greatest defense is their speed, as most mature hares can outrun the animals that hunt them. They are built with a fine-tuned early warning system to alert them that danger is near—large ears that pick up even the softest sounds, large eyes that take in a full circle's view around them, and sensitive noses that easily pick up scents at a distance.

Hares are also born with an impressive camouflage system. Arctic hares are a perfect example of the way an animal blends in with its environment for protection. Their tawny gray-brown summer coats match the earthy tones of the ground around them. As winter approaches, this short fur is replaced with a coat of thick, long, and very warm white hair. Even a wolf might miss a well-hidden white arctic hare lying still against a background of snow.

These animals also keep their populations strong by "breeding like rabbits." By the age of six months, a female hare is fully capable of giving birth to large litters (up to eight offspring) as often as four times a year.

Wolves do not depend on hares and rabbits as a main source of food, but will readily take them in when available, largely in the summer months.

Moose

speeds of fifteen miles per hour (24kph) in the water. Even calves can swim when only a few weeks old.

For this reason, if moose choose to flee from wolves, they often seek safety in water. With their long legs and strong lungs, they can also give a good chase on land—running thirty-five miles per hour (56.5kph) or more over long distances.

Still, healthy moose that stand their ground have the best success in defending themselves against wolves. They are, in fact, the most dangerous of the wolf's prey. Its height and strength make the moose's legs and hooves formidable weapons. The sharp-edged hooves are used like sledgehammers to kill or cripple an attacking wolf. To find success in securing fresh moose for dinner, wolves most often take old, sick, or disabled animals, or young calves that have become separated from their mothers.

BEAVERS

A full-grown beaver can weigh fifty to sixty pounds (23 to 27kg) and reach three to four feet (0.9 to 1.2) long, including its nearly foot (30.5cm) long tail. Add to that a tough hide, a protective layer of body fat, and formidable front teeth, and the beaver is no easy prey.

Beavers are mostly nocturnal creatures that work hard when the sun goes down. Much of that work is devoted to the building of their lodges—and beavers are truly master builders, creating dams and massive lodges for their families.

They depend on their highly developed senses of hearing and smell to warn them of danger, particularly when they go ashore. If a predator such as a wolf should approach, their best plan is to escape underground and underwater to the safety of their lodges. Beavers dig long tunnels, or plunge holes, that reach from underwater entrances to land, as far as thirty feet (9m) from shore. The forest entrances are hidden by vegetation. If cut off from the water's edge by a wolf or other predator, the beaver literally goes underground, escaping through a plunge hole beneath the forest floor.

With their superb swimming skills, beavers usually escape easily once in the water. They can dive deep and swim distances of up to half a mile (0.8km) to safety.

BISON

Long ago, bison traveled across North America by the thousands in great thundering herds. This huge mass of animals seemed to appear on the horizon from a thick cloud of dust that followed them. As large as they are, bison can still run fast—keeping up a pace of thirty-five miles per hour (56.5kph) for as long as half an hour—and can change direction almost instantly.

The bison (*Bison bison*) were an important source of food for wolves and for the Native Americans who lived on the rich grasslands of the plains. Native Americans learned much from wolves on how to effectively hunt the giant bison. One of George Catlin's most

famous oil paintings, *Buffalo Hunt Under the Wolf-Skin Mask*, depicts several Plains hunters dressed in the skins of wolves sneaking up on a herd of bison.

Skill was, indeed, a prerequisite for hunting bison, for both wolves and the Native Americans. An adult bull can weigh up to two thousand pounds (908kg), females up to the one-thousand pound (454kg) mark. The cows are only slightly shorter than the bulls, who may reach heights of six and a half feet (2m) at the shoulder. Even calves that start out at thirty to forty pounds (13.5 to 18kg) at birth tip the scales at four hundred to five hundred pounds (181.5 to 227kg) by one year.

Bison can smell trouble from afar, and when threatened, they use their heads. And rightly so—bison horns are twenty-two to twenty-six inches (56 to 66cm) long and as wide as two and a half feet (76cm) from tip to tip. An opponent faced with the massive bulk of one or more charging bison had best be alert.

Even with their incredible strength, formidable weapons, and great numbers, the bison could not defend themselves against the guns that came to the plains with the settlers. During the 1800s, thousands and thousands of bison were shot, as were wolves, and the plains began to change drastically. Fences began to appear on the grasslands as if they grew there, and cattle grazed much of the lands the bison once reigned.

When the bison's numbers had dropped from millions to fewer than a thousand, and the only wild bison remained in Yellowstone National Park and in Canada, people began to realize these great creatures could soon become extinct. Work to save the bison began, and today there are thousands.

WILD BOARS

It is natural that wild boars and wolves would meet in the Old World, because at one time, large populations of both shared much of the same wooded habitat. The European wild boar (*Sus scrofa*), for instance, with its numerous subspecies and races, ranges throughout Europe and the Middle East, to India, Asia, Japan, and most of North Africa.

Musk Ox

Most wild pigs are active in the evening or at night. Their acute sense of smell helps warn them of danger, and their thick skin and dense layer of fat are not easy for a wolf to penetrate if it is even successful in getting the chance. Wild pigs will defend themselves tenaciously, and all come equipped with an intimidating set of continually growing tusks. These tusks are used for food gathering and by males in rutting battles. Kept razor sharp by continuous wear of the upper tusks against the lower set, they present a formidable means of defense.

WILD SHEEP

Some of the species of sheep favored by wolves are mouflon *(Ovis orientalis)*; Rocky Mountain, or bighorn, sheep *(Ovis canadensis)*; and Dall's sheep *(Ovis dalli)*. No small prey, a mature Dall's sheep weighs more than a wolf at 180 to 200 pounds (82 to 91kg), and stands thirty-eight to forty inches (96.5 to 101.5cm) tall at the shoulder. Its greatest defense is to escape to steep slopes that are not easily accessible to wolves. Scaling steep cliffs is easy for an animal like a bighorn sheep. Their hooves have special pads that help them cling to rough and smooth surfaces alike. Wild sheep stay in small

herds and scan their surroundings carefully with eyes that can move independently in different directions.

MUSK OXEN

The average weight of a musk oxen *(Ovibos moschatus)* reaches seven hundred pounds (318kg), though they can weigh more. To protect themselves from attacking wolves, these massive beasts will form a circle with the young animals in the center. The adults face outward to protect their flanks and their young. They present to their adversaries a circle of formidable horns and heavy, slashing hooves.

GOAT ANTELOPES

There's much truth in the saying that there is safety in numbers. Animals such as Rocky Mountain goats *(Oreamnos americanus)* and chamois *(Rupicapra rupicapra)* generally live in small herds, with two or more animals always on the alert for approaching danger. Their best defense is their ability to manuever among rocky mountainsides and cliffs where predators dare not follow.

Efficient Eaters

To survive, wolves must rely on an arsenal of weapons, including sharp wits and sharp teeth, including the canine teeth, which get their name from these powerful animals.

The four canine teeth are an important part of the wolf's mouthful of forty-two teeth. These long, slightly curved teeth grow two to two and a half inches (5 to 6.5cm) from root to tip and allow the wolf to seize and hold on to its prey. The carnassial teeth, a set of upper premolars and lower molars located toward the back of the mouth, are specialized to shear through meat, skin, muscle, and connective tissue, slicing it into pieces that are easy to swallow. The wolf's incisors, too, are relatively large and slightly curved. This helps the wolf hold and tear the carcass to strip shreds of meat from the bone. The molars help crush and macerate bones and meat. In all, the upper jaw holds twenty teeth, the lower jaw twenty-two.

Long jaw muscles allow wolves to exert amazing pressure equaling fifteen hundred pounds (681kg) per square inch (twice as much as German shepherds). This kind of power is enough to break open even large leg bones easily, permitting wolves to get at the rich marrow. The wolf's digestive system is perfectly adapted to process pieces of bone, which are indigestible. Inside the digestive tract the bits of bone are swaddled in a protective covering of hair from the prey so that sharp edges can't puncture the soft intestines.

Wolves are very efficient feeders, consuming as much of their prey as they can, usually leaving only skull, large bones, and some hide and hair. What little is left is quickly cleaned up by scavengers such as eagles, foxes, and ravens. Wolves may also cache or bury food to be consumed later.

Well adapted to a feast-or-famine existence, the wolf is designed to fast for as long as two weeks while maintaining enough energy to continue its search for vulnerable prey. When the hunt is successful, wolves may gorge—each eating up to twenty pounds of meat (9kg) at a time. Their digestive systems process great quantities of meat quickly. While a large liver and pancreas help this process, it is important that wolves drink copious amounts of water to prevent uremic poisoning—a buildup of toxins in the blood associated with diets high in meat. That's one of the reasons wolves always live and travel close to water. The musculature of its tongue allows the wolf to curve the tip like a ladle to lap up water quickly.

Once wolves have gorged themselves fully, they may become "meat drunk." Full and almost in a daze, they sprawl out on their sides for a long nap if the sun is shining. If it's cold and windy or very snowy, they may curl up in a protected area, but the outcome is the same—the pack sleeps for several hours. For animals that spend a third of their lives in pursuit of food, catching up on a little rest is a necessary reward.

ABOVE: Wolves rarely let any part of a kill go to waste, and typically all that remains of a carcass after a feast are a few bones and scraps of fur. Wolves will also crack bones open to reach the marrow inside.

Making Your Mark

Wolves use a number of methods to communicate with one another. Vocalizations, body language, and scent marking all convey vital information, messages, and emotions.

Scent marking is important in clearly marking territorial boundaries and rights to food within those boundaries. Wolves have scent glands between their toes that allow them to leave their mark wherever they go. But urine marking is also an important method of posting messages and creating boundary maps.

Because of their keen sense of smell, wolves can learn a great deal about their environment and about other creatures through the odors they leave behind. Pack members can recognize the scents of their own pack mates' urine as distinctive from those belonging to wolves outside their pack.

Wolves purposefully mark trail junctions, tree stumps, and other highly visible sites, particularly areas where they share a common territorial border with a rival pack. Sometimes packs maintain buffer zones between territorial boundaries. Deer and other prey animals, and even lone wolves, make great use of these unoccupied safety zones to avoid confrontation with resident wolf packs.

Established travel routes are inspected and marked on a regular basis (on average once every three weeks) and scent marking is more frequent near borders. An alpha animal on the move will scent mark or inspect a scent mark as frequently as every two minutes. A dominant male will often underline or empha-size his message by scraping the area beside the urine mark with his foot.

Marking and defending territories is important because the wolf pack depends on a regular food supply for its survival. It must be assured of the use of a hunting area that has not been depleted of prey by another pack.

The size of wolf territories varies depending on pack size, climate, and terrain as well as on the relative abundance of prey animals and whether or not these animals migrate or stay in one area throughout the year. Territories vary, then, from fifty square miles (129.5 sq km) to thousands of square miles, or from approximately ten to five hundred square (26 to 1,295 sq km) miles per wolf. Sometimes territories remain constant for years if food supplies don't fluctuate too much.

Sense-abilities

Wolves use their sense of smell to locate prey more than any other method. Biologists' estimates vary, claiming wolves can detect scents anywhere from a hundred, a thousand, and even a million times better than humans. The human nose is equipped with approximately five million olfactory cells; members of the canid family have more than two hundred million. With the right wind conditions, wolves can pick up the scent of their prey one to one and a half miles (1.6 to 2.5km) away, and can smell objects buried deep

76

beneath the snow. Wolves also reap more information from the scents they gather than we can imagine—they can tell how many animals are traveling together, how many are males and how many are females, how long ago they passed by, and whether they are friend or foe. Their world, like that of many other animals, is rich with scents and sounds that we can never experience.

Wolves also have a far keener sense of hearing than humans. They can hear extraordinarily high pitches, such as the frequencies produced by bats and porpoises.

Not only can they hear sounds such as howls six miles (9.5km) away, and possibly as far as ten miles (16km) under the right conditions, but they can discriminate between tones that to our ears sound the same.

Wolves use all their senses to size up their prey. They process what they see quickly and with great accuracy. Their remarkable ability to detect moving objects over long distances, their acute peripheral vision, and their strong night vision are all keys to the success of these largely nocturnal predators.

OPPOSITE AND ABOVE: Traveling through their territory, wolves scent mark in highly visible locations such as along main trail junctions, on tree stumps, or around a successful kill. The scent mark provides a warning to potential intruders on the pack's territory and a welcome mat for returning members of the resident pack. Wolf pack territories are dynamic, and may sometimes overlap. Scent marking is more frequent in areas where the pack's territory borders that of a rival pack. Territories average about ten square miles (26 sq km) per adult wolf, but range between twenty-five and a thousand square miles (64.5 to 2,590 sq km) depending on a variety of environmental factors. Prey density is a key element, and where abundant prey populations are more stable, so are pack territories. Tundra wolves, however, have vast and elastic territories that allow these more nomadic wolves to follow the migratory patterns of their prey.

A Coat of Many Colors

No two wolves have exactly the same coat color or pattern. This is one way to tell one wolf from another. The colors of fur vary more in the wolf than in almost any other animal: coats range in color from snow white, cream, and buff to chestnut, brown, and black. Shades of light gray to charcoal predominate, which is why "gray wolf" is the common name for *Canis lupus*.

But even gray wolves are not solid gray. A wolf that looks gray has many colors of fur in its coat. Every hair that makes up the outer coat is multicolored. White, black, gray, and brown hairs are all blended together, giving the coat a distinct salt-and-pepper appearance. Usually the darkest colors are concentrated on the back, stretching from the head to the tip of the tail.

The wolf's coat is remarkably thick and luxurious in the winter months. The heavy coat is divided into "capes" of long, glossy guard hairs that shed rain and snow and help keep the wolf dry. A dense underfur provides insulation to keep the wolf warm. Wolves usually shed this light-colored, downy underfur during the hotter months.

The wolf's extraordinary fur allows it to live rather comfortably in cold climates. As protection against bitter cold and wet, the coat grows particularly thick across the shoulders, and guard hairs in this area may be up to five inches (12.5cm) long. A wolf's fur is unusual in that ice will not accumulate on the fur when warm, moist breath condenses against it. When a wolf nestles its muzzle and nose between its rear legs and covers them with the thick insulation of its fluffy tail, it can turn its back against the wind and sleep peacefully in weather that drops to -40 or -50°F (-40 or -45.5°C).

RIGHT: Many wolves living in the far North have beautiful white coats. The white hairs are hollow, which permits air to collect in the shafts, insulating the animal against the cold. **OVERLEAF:** Wolves of all ages enjoy some time to play. Wolf games include tag, pouncing, tumbling, wrestling, and keep-away (using any treasured "toy," including a stick, bone, pine cone, antler, or even a piece of hide).

Chapter 5

All in the Family— Life in the Wolf Pack

WE LISTENED FOR A VOICE CRYING IN THE WILDERNESS.

AND WE HEARD THE JUBILATION OF WOLVES!

—DURWARD L. ALLEN

Social Bonds

A successful hunt depends on the cooperative efforts of the entire pack. It is vital that all members get along and understand their roles if the pack is to survive. They depend on one another to bring down the game that would certainly elude them if each worked alone.

A well-understood and respected hierarchy eliminates most serious conflict within the pack. Wolves are incredibly strong, and potential injuries could be fatal if wolves chose to fight one another. Hunting would be less efficient without the full strength of each individual, and the pack would suffer.

Wolves possess a strong social nature. The pack is a family of related animals with a mated pair at its head. The other members of the group are generally their offspring of several years—subordinate adults, juveniles, and pups.

Pack size varies depending on the size and availability of prey. Wolves that hunt relatively small animals can survive in packs of as few as three. To hunt deer regularly, a pack of at least six is more efficient. Large and dangerous prey such as moose and wild boar require large packs of skilled hunters. Packs with as many as twenty to thirty members have been documented, though it is rare to find packs much larger than twelve. Typically, six to eight family members comprise a wolf pack.

Understanding this sophisticated and highly complex social unit and its dynamics is the key to understanding wolves. Each wolf assumes a particular role within the pack—a role that may change as the wolf

matures and develops into either a strong, decisive animal or, perhaps, a more submissive follower.

THE HIERARCHY

THE ALPHA PAIR Male and female leaders of the pack

YOUNG SUBORDINATES Males and females, including the beta wolf (the second-ranking male)

JUVENILES AND PUPS Both sexes

THE OMEGA WOLF Male or female scapegoat (bears the brunt of the pack's frustrations and harassment and may be the last to feed or will go without when food is scarce)

The alpha male and female are usually the oldest and most experienced members of the pack. They are confident, decisive, and outgoing. The alpha male and female guide the activities of the pack and share the duties of leadership; the alpha male may determine hunting strategies and take the initiative in marking his pack's territorial boundaries. The alpha female makes decisions on where to establish den sites—a crucial role, as this determines where the pack will live and hunt during the mating and breeding season and for a month or more after the pups are born.

Most often, but not always, the alpha male and female are the only wolves to breed, prohibiting all other wolves in the pack from mating. During the mating season and throughout the time the pups are in the den, the alpha female holds the most dominant role within the pack.

Dominant wolves display strong, even aggressive, personalities and must be confident decision makers. Alpha leaders have to be able to earn the respect and affection of other pack members. Lower-ranking members show this respect by approaching the alpha male or female with their bodies lowered and greeting them by reaching up to lick or nuzzle the alpha animal's face. "Top dog" in the wolf pack is an honored role and even young pups begin testing and challenging one another through play fighting to establish dominance.

Alpha animals not only act like leaders, they look like leaders, too. They carry their bodies with confidence, standing tall with tail held high or out straight and ears erect. They always look other animals directly in the eye. Clear communication is a key element to the success of a cooperative pack—when communications from the alpha animal are clear and are respected by other pack members, disputes can be settled quickly and without physical confrontation. Wolves communicate even complex messages in very subtle ways. A quelling glance

OPPOSITE AND ABOVE: Parents are particularly attentive to their pups, but all members of the pack share in rearing wolf pups once they have left the den. Pups learn to greet adults with friendly, if somewhat anxious, licks on the muzzle. This serves more than one purpose. When pups are young, whining and licking or nipping at an adult's muzzle may elicit a feeding response. As pups mature, this mouth nuzzling becomes a display of the subordinate affection that pack members other than alpha wolves display throughout their lives. **OVERLEAF:** Within the pack, confrontations between two individuals rarely spread any further. The visual vocabulary of body movements and facial expressions conveys everything these wolves need to communicate to settle this dispute swiftly and safely.

or a quick growl may be all that is necessary to keep the peace. Even when pack members don't see eye to eye, quarrels are quickly forgotten once settled.

So strong is the wolf pack's complex social structure that the untimely death of an alpha leader can cause major difficulties and changes within the pack. Some shuffling of roles is part of the natural order of things, as alpha wolves grow old and are overthrown by younger, stronger animals, but wolf packs that undergo losses of strong leaders in their prime—particularly through consistent human persecution—may find their social structure unraveling. Subordinate pack members need time to learn the skills their leaders can teach. The health of a wolf pack cannot be measured in sheer numbers but rather by the strength and skills brought to the whole pack by individuals, each playing an integral role.

A wolf's decision to leave the security of the pack is not made lightly, as a lone wolf is quite vulnerable. Wolves are usually quite hostile toward any wolf outsiders and will even kill lone wolves that trespass across territorial boundaries. In addition, acquiring food is a

dangerous and difficult proposition for a whole pack, much less a wolf on its own.

When they do disperse, wolves are most likely to do so during the winter courtship and breeding season or in the spring when the pack size expands with a new litter. Often it is confident and aggressive wolves under the age of two that choose to become dispersers and possibly leaders of their own packs. They may leave because they have been harassed by other pack members, because food supplies have become scarce in their pack's territory, or because of a need to mate that cannot be fulfilled within their pack of origin.

Male and female lone wolves may survive long enough to meet and pair up to establish their own territory either within the buffer zones that separate established wolf pack territories or within the boundaries of territories that are no longer in use. Those animals that do not disperse are known as biders—wolves that literally bide their time hoping to advance in the hierarchy and possibly take over alpha positions when the current leaders die or become too old to head the pack.

ABOVE: While the breeding season typically begins in late winter, the tension over dominance may begin much earlier, in late autumn or early in the winter. The alpha female will often launch a campaign against her rivals— the other adult females of the pack—attempting to temporarily exclude them from the pack so that she may remain the only breeding female. Once the season has begun, the alpha male will likewise make every effort to prevent rival males from mating with the alpha female, or indeed with any other adult female.

The Call of the Wild

Different sounds, or vocalizations, convey a variety of messages. Wolves growl, yelp, whine, snarl, squeal, squeak, bark, whimper, and howl. Deep-throated growling implies a threat, while barking (relatively infrequent in wolves) serves to signal alarm. Whining and whimpering are usually soft, high-pitched, friendly greeting sounds, and are usually associated with feeding pups or with play. Vocalizations most often accompany and emphasize or clarify facial and body gestures.

Of course, the wolf's trademark vocalization is its evocative, hauntingly beautiful howl or, more rightly, howls. Subtle nuances distinguish one type of howl from another, and wolves know the differences between the various types of howls even when humans don't.

Howling celebrates the unity of the pack. Wolves use howls to reinforce their claim to their territory, particularly when rival wolves are nearby. Because each wolf has its own distinctive voice and howls on a different note, their chorus gives the impression of many more wolves howling than there truly are. Some biologists suggest this may serve an important function in defending the pack's territory. When a pack of three wants to sound like a pack of eight, the wolves don't all howl on the same note or they may sound like a pack of one.

Wolves sometimes howl to reunite the pack—whether they have actually been physically separated in their travels or simply to rediscover one another after a long sleep. As they awaken and greet one another or as they gear up for a hunt, their howls reinforce their commitment to one another and to the pack. Each member of the pack can be identified by the others from its own distinctive call. Sometimes wolves howl, apparently, for the sheer pleasure of howling. This joyful chorus is what wildlife biologist Durward Allen aptly termed "the jubilation of wolves."

Wolves do not, contrary to legend, howl at the moon, and their howling is no more excited during a full moon than on any other night. Howling tends to be more frequent in the cool of evening and in early morning hours when wolves are most active. That the moon is more visible during those hours has little to do with the wolf's song. Wolves may seem to lift their voices to the sky because they usually raise their muzzles as they howl. This body posture makes sense, since the call is intended to carry a great distance through the air.

Body posture and facial expressions have a lot to do with the way wolves communicate. Among the clearest symbols of a wolf's dominance within the pack is the way

ABOVE: Howling helps wolves keep track of the pack and claim their territory, and encourages camaraderie. Each individual wolf in the pack has a distinctive voice, and when the pack howls together, they harmonize. **OVERLEAF:** One member of the pack usually begins a group howl and the others then join in, each on a different note. This joyous howling is kept to a minimum near a den when the pack has young pups to protect. Adults are careful not to draw attention to a mother and her pups in their vulnerable state.

it carries its tail. Most pack members carry their long, bushy tails hanging down; an alpha wolf, however, is usually seen with its tail held high, like a banner.

In the most submissive or frightened posture, a wolf will actually tuck its tail between its legs. Low-ranking pack members also keep their ears low and laid back in submission, while alpha members look alert and confident with their ears erect. Ears up also signifies friendship and readiness for play, while ears laid close beside the head usually indicates aggression or fear.

These "tell-tail" signs are reinforced with complementary body and facial signals as well as with vocalizations. This kind of clear communication, even when aggressive in nature, serves the pack well in keeping harmony among its members. A threat display, for instance, may be a way for a wolf to let off steam without actually following through with a fight. A strong message received with respect is all that's necessary to assert

ABOVE: How a wolf uses body language is determined by its place in the pack structure and by the situation at hand. Here, an alpha wolf with tail held high and ears erect makes sure a subordinate clearly understands its place. **OPPOSITE:** Confrontations such as this rarely turn into physical conflict. It simply doesn't make sense to hurt a member of the pack because the group depends on each individual to hunt, and so to survive. Conflict is avoided by using succinct gestures and facial expressions. Threats are conveyed through bared teeth, fixed stares, growls, raised ears, and wrinkled brows. Submission, on the other hand, is clearly understood when a wolf flattens its ears, lowers its head and tail, or even drops to the ground and rolls over in a most vulnerable posture.

authority. It's unwise to let confrontations escalate further when the individual that could be hurt is a relative, a mate, or offspring whose help in the hunt is crucial for the health and survival of the entire pack. Instead, wolves maximize the message to minimize the costs in injury.

Much of the communication among wolves is congenial and happy. When greeting another member of the pack or inviting others to play, wolves wag their tails happily and even pull back their lips in what resembles a grin. It is easy to recognize the difference between a tense, aggressive body posture and the relaxed movements of a happy, playful wolf. Adults and pups alike enjoy a good chase and tumble.

Wolves' expressive faces paint a clear picture of how they feel. There is no better warning than a dominant wolf's impressive bared teeth accompanied by a low growl, especially if it crouches as if to lunge at the offending party.

The answer also comes back loud and clear when the threatened wolf rolls over on the ground with its belly or side exposed in a vulnerable and conciliatory posture.

The wolf's markings accentuate its expressions. Its eyes draw immediate attention because they are outlined in black and are often at least partially surrounded by lighter fur. Its jet black nose stands out against a long muzzle, which is commonly white on the sides all the way to the cheeks. Dark markings in the center of the ears and around the outer edges stand out and highlight expressions. Even the lips are lined in black, making a grin or bared teeth appear more prominent.

A wolf's body language is also exaggerated by the color and use of its fur—a wolf can raise the hair along its neck and shoulders. This behavior, called "raising the hackles," makes the wolf appear much larger, and therefore more threatening, than normal.

Pups in the Pack

Late winter is the time for breeding. Depending on the latitude, this season falls sometime between late January and April. The higher the latitude, the later the breeding season. A gestation period of sixty-three days means wolf pups are born sometime between March and June, when food is easier to obtain. In the colder northern areas especially, the timing of the breeding season is crucial, so many young are born during the spring or early summer when survival is favored. Pups born during plentiful times will have the best chance to grow strong before the cold and snow of winter arrive again.

During the mating season, the breeding pair (almost always the alpha male and female only) are especially close and affectionate. The female is in heat for only five to seven days, and mating may occur several times during this period. The dominant pair is likely to use its social advantages to keep other pack members from mating and thus control overpopulation.

When the breeding pair mates, the male mounts the female from behind. An actual physical tie occurs during copulation, caused by the swelling of the bulb of the male's penis and the constriction of the muscles in the female's vaginal wall. The penis is virtually held in place, preventing withdrawal for as long as twenty to thirty minutes.

Once the female is pregnant, the pack has nine weeks to prepare for the birth of the pups—and they all participate in some way. Like most pack activities, the birth and care of pups is a group effort. A growing excitement sweeps through the pack as preparations get under way. While the alpha female begins to prepare one or more dens, the other pack members store food for her to eat, burying it in caches near the den site. They dig these underground storage areas with their feet and use their noses to cover the meat with dirt.

The pregnant female may create a den in a cave, a hollow log, or an abandoned den of another animal, such as a beaver or fox. The most common den, however, is a burrow the female digs herself in the soft, sandy dirt of a hillside. The small oval entrance is just large enough for the adult to go through. A narrow, upward-sloping tunnel ten to thirty feet (3 to 9m) in length connects the burrow's entrance to the birth chamber, where the pups will live for their first few weeks. The upward slope helps prevent rainwater from reaching the chamber.

ABOVE: Young pups have small ears, large heads with blunt muzzles, and thin tails. Their coats are a soft, fuzzy brown and, like human babies, most are born with blue eyes. As the pups grow, their coats become coarser and change in color; littermates may end up with widely different markings. When they are between eight and sixteen weeks of age, most young wolves' eyes begin to change to a golden color. By six months of age the pups look like slightly smaller versions of adult wolves, and can be hard to distinguish from older pack members. **OPPOSITE:** In addition to helping develop crucial survival skills, wolf pup play is clearly just plain fun.

Requirements for a suitable den site include a dry, elevated, secure area within good hunting territory and situated close to a fresh water source. This is important because from the time the den site is chosen until the end of summer, the life of the pack will revolve around this area. If an area remains undisturbed, the same den may be used for several years. Often the female will prepare more than one den as a backup site, in case environmental conditions or encroaching animals threaten the pups.

A new den may be complete as early as three weeks before the pups are due to arrive, and is kept painstakingly clean. A day or so before the birth of the pups, the female enters the confinement of the den.

The birth of five or six pups to a litter is common, though as few as two or as many as ten to eleven is possible. Mortality rates are as high as 60 percent for young pups. Weighing only one pound (454g) each and helpless at birth, wolf pups cannot see or hear and cannot regulate their own body temperatures. They depend completely on their mother for food, warmth, and protection in their first few weeks of life, and do not leave the safety of the den. Their mother is the only member of the pack that has contact with the pups during this time.

All pups are covered with a fine, woolly brown fur at birth, though littermates may grow up with coats of varying tones. They have small, floppy ears, rounded heads, and pug noses.

Within two weeks of birth, pups open their baby blue eyes. Only a few will keep this hue, as eye colors usually change to shades of amber, brown, gold, and green as pups mature. At about the time they open their eyes, wolf pups also begin to walk. They have grown quickly

Growing pups can explore and play safely at a rendezvous site, even while the adults are away hunting. Usually at least one adult will stay behind as a pup sitter. Small meadows ringed with trees and brush and close to water make perfect rendezvous sites; while they wait for the rest of the pack, the pups can build the coordination and strength that will help them as adults by climbing, jumping, running, and tumbling.

on a rich, high-fat diet of their mother's milk, and by three weeks begin to eat semisolid food regurgitated by their mother. A week later, they will be ready to venture outside to the entrance of the den.

The excitement among the pack is hard to contain as the wolves greet, sniff, nuzzle, and lick the pups. Much tail wagging ensues as the youngest relatives—the pack's future—are welcomed into the family.

Raising the pups now truly becomes a group effort as each wolf takes on a role of caregiver—as food provider, playmate, pup sitter, or protective guardian. Now, adult wolves carry food back to the pups, announcing their arrival with little squeaking noises. They are greeted with a rush of hungry, squeaking, begging, tail-wagging pups who nibble and lick the feeders' muzzles to stimulate regurgitation. Growing wolf pups require two to three times more food per pound (454g) of weight than do adults for energy, warmth, and healthy growth. Eating, sleeping, and playing fill the pups' days. Affectionate and tolerant, the adults put up with the pups' playful antics, sometimes even joining in.

Chasing, stalking, play-fighting, pouncing, romping, running, and chewing on anything and everything occupies a pup's attention throughout the time it is awake. In addition to entertainment, this play is the beginning of skills development that will be important as the young wolf grows. These activities help the pups build coordination and strength and are also a part of a young wolf's socialization; the pups are, in effect, imitating adult wolves. And, perhaps most importantly, the pups develop close relationships with one another and with other members of their family, helping to maintain the pack's cohesiveness and establishing each pup's role in the dominance hierarchy.

By the time they are six weeks old, curious pups try to follow the adults for short distances from the den. They are not yet old enough to follow far or to venture out on their own. Pups love to explore the world around them, taking care not to stray too far from the den site. They show the greatest interest in blades of grass, fallen leaves, and pieces of bone. They eagerly gallop behind adult wolves as if to shadow them, chase small animals (especially birds), pounce on twigs, and splash in puddles. Though they have less speed, stamina, and strength than adults, the pups are learning important skills to help them survive in the wild.

Bold pups will climb all over an adult, pulling its tail and nipping its ears—as long as the adult will tolerate these antics, that is. Adult wolves are very gentle, loving, and patient with playful pups. Even older pack members will romp with the pups and take part in a game of tag or join the whole pack for a joyful howl. No matter what its age, a wolf's outstanding qualities include friendliness, curiosity, and intelligence.

By the time wolf pups are eight to ten weeks old, they have developed enough to leave the den site and join the pack at the rendezvous site. This area, still within the pack's territory, is about an acre (0.4ha) in size and is always near water. The move gives the pups their first feel for the wide-ranging, roaming life of the wolf—a life not too far off for them. Here they will spend their days continuing to develop their skills, exploring, playing, and sleeping under the watchful care of a relative who acts a pup sitter while the other adults hunt. Sometimes, the same rendezvous site is used by the pack as their summer social center for several years in a row.

As autumn approaches and the young wolves reach six months of age, they show signs of development that indicate they can travel with the pack, although at a slightly slower pace. The wolves are, once again, on the move as a pack. The pack breaks its stride only for brief periods of feeding, rest, and play, until the winter breeding season is upon them again and the cycle begins anew.

Pups aren't physically mature until they are at least two years old. Successful breeding isn't likely, for those who become the dominant wolves of the pack, until they reach three years or more.

In the meantime, the pups follow the adults, learning to recognize their territory, to detect prey, and to hunt skillfully and efficiently. It's the role they were born to play in nature. If they do it well, they should rightfully survive, for they have no enemies in the wild.

TOP: What a prize. Three nine-week-old wolf pups vie for sole proprietorship of a rack of bones. At this stage, games and toys become clear tests not only of strength and coordination, but of developing social skills that help pups establish their own rank or levels of dominance among themselves. **ABOVE LEFT:** A bushy tail is the perfect target for a wolf pup's high level of energy. Despite such spirited antics, adult wolves are patient and affectionate with the pups and tolerant of their high jinks. **ABOVE RIGHT:** Big eyes highlight a wolf pup's face. As newborns, pups look almost more like tiny bear cubs than like wolves. Proportionately, they have smaller ears, shorter muzzles, and shorter legs than adult wolves. **OVERLEAF:** In the wild, wolves are often elusive and watchful—habits that, no doubt, have been the basis for many myths and legends surrounding the "mysterious" wolf.

On Common Ground

Only a mountain has lived long enough

to listen objectively to the howl of a wolf.

—Aldo Leopold

Face to Face

The wolf has only one enemy—but it is a formidable one. Long since removed from the wild, "civilized" man has forgotten much of what he once understood of the natural world. Fearful of the universe that lay within deep forests and across untamed prairies, man sought to dominate and harness it for his own use. The wolf stood in man's way.

The hunter who once respected the wolf's prowess now reviled it as a competitor. The herdsman feared and hated the wolf out of concern for the livestock that were his livelihood, and because of a cultural heritage that regarded the wolf as evil incarnate.

As early as 300 B.C., wolfhounds were bred by the Celts especially for killing wolves. Powerful and fast, the Irish wolfhound is the tallest dog breed in the world, standing up to thirty-five inches (89cm) at the shoulder. Used to hunt down its wild relatives, these massive dogs were considered so vital that in 1652, Oliver Cromwell forbade their export from Britain.

Around 800 A.D., the Emperor Charlemagne, called for a special order of army officers, the louvetiers. Their charge was to organize citizens for the sole purpose of hunting down and killing wolves.

Wolfmonat, or "wolf month," was the name for January in Anglo-Saxon England. It was the month specifically devoted to killing wolves.

Wolf hunting became a sporting leisure activity for the wealthy upper classes by the early sixteenth century. By the end of the 1800s the wolf had all but vanished from European soil: wolves were gone from Denmark by 1772 and from Ireland by 1821; a hunter in Scotland held the dubious honor of killing Britain's last wolf in 1848.

Poisoned by the hatred of wolves that had become a European tradition, early settlers in North America carried on the slaughter—often using true poisons as their weapon. The riches of the New World were many but, apparently, not enough to be

OPPOSITE AND ABOVE: As wolf recovery efforts succeed, some of us will be the beneficiaries, lucky enough to observe wild wolves at a relatively close range. Of course, there are attendant hazards for wolves when they live in close proximity to man; wolves in many recovery areas have been hit by cars. In some areas, this has been the most significant cause of death among reintroduced wolves. For wolf conservationists, the problems encountered when wolves are reintroduced too close to populated areas make it clear that we must set aside areas of relative wilderness if the wolf is to survive.

shared with wolves. As eastern forests began to yield to the pressures of civilization and farmsteads, the wolf did not. While its natural prey may have been diminished, its quest for survival was not. The wolf was bound to meet the farmer and his livestock on their own turf, and so was bound to eventually meet conflict as well.

Soon, the settlers' path would stretch farther and farther west. Lewis and Clark blazed a trail that was followed by fur trappers in search of valuable beaver pelts. But a shift in the fur market in the mid-1800s made bison, deer, elk, and wolves the main targets.

Clouds of dust rolled along the Great Plains and western ranges as the thundering herds of bison roamed. But as those clouds disappeared, the dust settled on a different land—a foreign land for the wolves. As the bison vanished so, too, would the wolves. The vast grasslands became home to farms and ranches and cities. Cattle and sheep replaced the bison. The war on wolves escalated to a magnitude of violence that today seems incomprehensible. Exact numbers we will never know, but records from the time provide a rough estimate of one to two million wolves annihilated during the last half of the nineteenth century.

Strychnine became a household item on farmsteads and ranches and a staple in the kit of every cowboy or "wolfer," as those who killed wolves for a living became known. In *Last of the Lions*, Stanley Young wrote, "There was a sort of unwritten law of the range that no cowman would knowingly pass by a carcass of any kind without inserting a good dose of strychnine, in hope of killing one or more wolf." Poisoning was the method of choice primarily because it proved most "efficient" in killing large numbers of wolves (and other animals) at one time. Over miles of prairie and rangeland, carcasses would be laced with heavy doses of poison and left to attract hungry victims.

The introduction of the steel leghold trap in the mid-1800s provided another reliable method of killing wolves. Practiced wolf trappers knew how to set a baited trap near fresh wolf kills, how to construct a "blind" trap covered with dirt along a wolf trail, or how to "scent paint" a trap with a mixture of animal parts and blood, feces, or urine, hiding it among brush or rocks. Once triggered, these traps clamp onto an animal's foot with strong metal jaws. The trap holds the limb so tightly that wolves have been known to chew through their own legs in desperate attempts to free themselves.

If poisons, traps, and guns could not exterminate the wolf quickly enough, humans only pushed the limits of invention further. Pups in their dens were dug up and strangled, flooded out, or destroyed with dynamite. Hounds were bred and trained specifically for their power, speed, and aggressiveness in hunting wolves. But perhaps most insidious was a method devised to capture wolves for the sole purpose of infecting them with sarcoptic mange and releasing them again. These carriers could then spread the debilitating parasitic disease throughout the wolf population.

In 1907 the government established the United States Biological Survey, with extermination of the wolf as the organization's foremost objective. To this end, the U.S. government hired three hundred full-time hunters and trappers to serve as predator control agents; the agency also offered bounties for dead wolves to "free-lance" wolf killers. The majority of the country—from government officials to farmers—agreed that the wolf should be eradicated.

Without their habitat, their natural prey, or a respite from the continuous onslaught, wolves could not hang on. Face to face, finally, with their only true enemy, a scant few wolves managed to survive to 1930. Of those that eluded their pursuers the longest, a handful became legendary in their own right. These outlaws that would not be brought to justice were both reviled for their crimes and renowned for their courage and cunning. Interestingly, many of these wily wolves were crippled or injured. Hunting slow-moving livestock instead of the more fleet-footed wild prey may have been their only hope for survival. They did not, after all, recognize those animals as someone else's property.

THE OUTLAWS

Outlaw wolves became frontier characters with names and stories of their own.

It was the nature writer Ernest Thompson Seton who wrote about finally subduing Lobo, King of the Currumpaw, and his mate Blanca of northern New Mexico. Only after many attempts using poisons and traps did Blanca eventually succumb, dying a painful and gruesome death, literally pulled apart by her captors. Using Blanca's body as bait, Seton trapped Lobo not once, as the tale goes, but four times. With a trap on each of his four feet, Lobo still struggled to free himself, glaring at Seton, until the wolf exhausted himself. It was only then that Seton forced a stick through Lobo's mouth, tied his jaws, placed a collar around his neck, and staked him alone in a field. The next day, the mighty King of the Currumpaw was dead.

Old Lefty, Three Toes, and Las Margaritas were all infamous wolves who had lost part or all of a foot in a trap. Old Lefty traveled the area around Burns Hole, Colorado. Stories from Harding County, South Dakota, claim that it took thirteen years and 150 hunters and trappers to stop the marauding Three Toes. It took the famous trapper Roy McBride eleven months of concentrated effort and thousands of miles on horseback crossing the Mexican states of Durango and Zacatecas to pursue Las Margaritas.

The Ghost Wolf of the Judith Basin in Montana during the 1920s was even more crafty. She avoided traps strewn throughout the area, continued even after hunters shot her in the hind leg, and even held her own against five

imported Russian wolfhounds. A bullet finally killed the Ghost Wolf in 1930.

Even an old, deaf wolf outsmarted hunters and trappers for years in Texas, where killing the White Lobo became so important that a five-hundred-dollar bounty was placed on her head.

A five-hundred-dollar bounty was also the incentive that brought about the demise of Old Aquila. After years of "taunting" hunters and trappers, she was poisoned in 1924.

Notorious legends grew around these crafty, elusive wolves. When one was finally killed, celebrations, banquets, parades, and retellings of lofty exploits were the order of the day. More than once, such occasions were marked by the presentation of an award to the killer, such as an engraved gold watch.

And so it was that the howls of the last wolves in what had once been a vast wilderness were silenced.

In their pursuit of progress, humans destroyed the wolf's natural prey and laid barren its rich habitats. In place of forests and open prairies rife with deer and buffalo, man fenced fields and filled them with grazing livestock. With these now plentiful herbivores virtually their only food source—their only real chance for survival—wolves naturally took advantage. People, in turn, waged war on the wolf.

By about 1900 the wolf was absent from the eastern half of the United States (except for the area around the Great Lakes). On the Great Plains, the wolf was exterminated by 1926. In Canada, the wolf was little seen in the east by the 1870s, and was extinct by 1880 in New Brunswick, by 1900 in Nova Scotia, and by 1913 in Newfoundland. Washington State heard its last wolf howl in 1940, and both Colorado and Wyoming killed their last wolves in 1943.

Gone is the wolf from nearly 95 percent of its original range in the United States—the largest population is currently in Alaska, where it is still hunted and trapped. The wolf has likewise disappeared from more than 15 percent of its original range in Canada, surviving mostly in the northern areas, and there, too, it continues to be hunted and trapped. In Mexico the wolf has fared even worse—it is most likely extinct throughout its entire original range there.

Extinct in nearly all of Europe, including Belgium, Denmark, England, Ireland, Scotland, Wales, Liechtenstein, Switzerland, Monaco, and the Netherlands, wolves have a stronghold (if somewhat tenuous) in the former Soviet Union, although they are still hunted and trapped.

Where wolf control still goes on today, both the reasoning and the methods often bring heated debate. Most wolf control on the eve of the twenty-first century is done with traps, snares, aerial hunting, and poisoning—by government personnel and by private hunters and trappers.

Regulations on trapping and snaring often require daily checks, but enforcement is extremely difficult. Animals left in traps or snares for many days die slow and painful deaths through starvation and freezing. Deer, moose, and many other animals that use the same trails often become caught in snares intended to choke wolves.

ABOVE: Stories of wolves attacking people are widely exaggerated. Certainly, the idea of assaults by massive packs of wolves, as depicted here in an engraving titled *The Russian Serf's Self-Sacrifice*, were created out of greatly embellished tales. Attacks in Europe many years ago are now generally attributed to rabid wolves or, more often, to wolf-dog hybrids. **OPPOSITE:** The terrifying image of wolves setting upon helpless travelers in the woods, which was fed by art such as this, helped to engender a widespread campaign to rid Europe of wolves altogether. They were trapped, shot, and poisoned in a war that, in some areas, is still waged today.

Aerial hunting of wolves with fixed-wing aircraft or helicopters first became popular in the 1940s. Because it requires the hunter to be able to track wolves for long distances, aerial hunting is generally done when the ground has a good snow cover and the wolves are more easily visible. This is the time, too, when hunters on snowmobiles pursue wolves. With the assistance of these vehicles, hunters can easily drive wolf packs to exhaustion—particularly on the open tundra, where cover is sparse.

While strychnine was the poison of choice in the Old West, cyanide and fluorine-acetate of barium later became prevalent. In the 1940s, the United States Armed Forces developed a poison known as compound 1080 to combat rats. This lethal weapon was quickly put to use in the war against wolves. Though wolves were, initially at least, the target, they weren't its only victims. Great numbers of coyotes, domestic dogs, and foxes were also killed.

Even as the last wolf survivors eked out a difficult living, there were a few people who began to see them in a different light. One, a young biologist named Adolph Murie, had a profound effect on how wildlife managers were to view predators, particularly wolves. His extensive study, later published as "The Wolves of Mount McKinley," examined wolf pack behaviors and wolves' relationships both with pack members and with other animals.

Murie's work was so highly regarded that, for a brief time at least, it persuaded the National Park Service to suspend a wolf control program in 1943 in Mount McKinley National Park (also known as Denali National Park). Antiwolf groups combined their strengths in a campaign to reinstate the wolf control program over the next few years.

It would not be the last time wolf control sparked controversy in Alaska or, indeed, in any of a number of places in North America.

BOUNTY AND THE BEAST

Bounties have abounded through the centuries to encourage the killing of wolves. In ancient Greece, as early as 600 B.C. there were bounties paid for dead wolves.

England placed a bounty on the wolf in the 1500s. The Massachusetts Bay Colony created the first North American wolf bounty in 1630. Jamestown, Virginia, and other colonies soon followed suit.

Cash and coin were not the only rewards—corn, tobacco, wine, and, ironically, livestock were some of the riches to be had. Native Americans might be paid in blankets for wolf pelts. In an odd twist, if they were unfortunate enough to come under the jurisdiction of South Carolina's Act for Destroying Beasts of Prey (1695), they were required annually to make payment of a wolf skin or skin of another predator. Those who did not make payment were whipped.

As settlers moved west, bounties moved with them. By the mid-1800s, the bounty system was a burgeoning business in which many a wolfer plied his trade and earned his living. Minnesota's first wolf bounty in 1849 paid three dollars per pelt.

The lesser fee of only one dollar per dead wolf under Montana's 1884 wolf bounty law still brought in 5,450 wolves the first year. During a period of only thirty-five years, more than eighty thousand wolves were turned in for bounty payments in Montana alone. Another thirty-six thousand wolf bounties were paid in Wyoming between

1895 and 1917. Arizona and New Mexico joined the wolf bounty wagon in 1893.

Not all bounties were paid by local and state governments. Stockmen's organiza-

ABOVE: A trapper in Canada meets with success. At one time, the gray wolf ranged throughout Canada and across almost all of the United States, including Alaska. Historic payments for wolf pelts have ranged from less than $1 per pelt in 1830 to $195 in the early 1990s. **OPPOSITE:** White Sands National Park, New Mexico. **PAGES 112–113:** Rolling and tumbling is good fun whether you're a pup or just a pup at heart.

tions and individual ranches also paid hefty rewards for the destruction of the animal they saw as their greatest enemy. By 1914, more than one million dollars was paid annually in predator bounties in the western states.

The wolfer's role took him into vast areas during the cold of winter, when wolf pelts were prime. For his clothing, cooking equipment, food, horses, wagon, poison, rifles, and skinning knife, an investment of about $150 was standard. During that three to four months of work, however, he might earn as much as three thousand dollars. He might also earn himself a place among the legends of the Old West.

Bounties did not disappear with the glory days of the Old West: they are very much with us today. Even though the proposals violate the Endangered Species Act, several states have recently taken a stand against the wolf:

WYOMING HOUSE BILL 214

This bill proposed that a five-hundred-dollar bounty be offered to hunters who killed wolves that strayed out of Yellowstone National Park during reintroduction efforts. Though it failed, it was quickly reintroduced at the higher rate of one thousand dollars and passed in the Senate before it was vetoed by Governor Gerringer.

ARIZONA HOUSE BILL 2548

A five-hundred-dollar bounty was proposed by those hoping to push federal officials to reconsider efforts to reintroduce the critically endangered Mexican wolf, a gray wolf subspecies, in areas of Arizona.

ALASKA SENATE BILL 81

The bill proposed a four-hundred-dollar cash bounty (which was later reduced to two hundred dollars) for killing wolves in Alaska "by any method or means without restriction." Wolves in Alaska are not listed as endangered and so do not have specific protection under federal law. In fact, the government sponsors programs under which wolves are hunted and trapped as big-game animals.

Return of the Wolf— Conflict, Controversy, and Celebration

WHAT IS MAN WITHOUT THE BEASTS?

IF ALL THE BEASTS WERE GONE,

MEN WOULD DIE FROM A GREAT LONELINESS OF SPIRIT.

FOR WHATEVER HAPPENS TO THE BEASTS,

SOON HAPPENS TO MAN.

ALL THINGS ARE CONNECTED.

—CHIEF SEATTLE

The Wolf in Our Own Backyard

Can wolves and humans coexist? In a word, yes.

But conscious decision on the part of humans is necessary in accepting the right of the wolf—or any animal—to exist.

People are passionate about wolves. That passion may be translated into hatred or idealism—and either can have negative effects for the wolf. The more we learn about the wolf, the more we come to understand its role in the ecosystem and in the world. There are sacrifices that humans must make to keep rivers and oceans, forests and wetlands, prairies and mountainsides healthy and fit to sustain animal life. There are many people today who believe those sacrifices are well worth making in order to preserve wilderness areas and the variety of plants and animals they hold.

Conservation is often rife with controversy and conflict. The long history of wolf hatred makes this particularly true for this wild predator.

THE GRAY WOLF

Canada

In Canada, home to one of the world's largest populations of wolves, the history of wolves has been marked with difficulties. Agricultural practices, apathy, persecution, and poorly enforced wildlife harvesting laws between 1900 and 1960 reduced the wolf's range and numbers. A change in attitudes during the past thirty years has brought wolves back to nearly 86 percent of their former range throughout Canada and its arctic islands, and on Vancouver Island. Current wolf population estimates range between fifty thousand and sixty thousand animals.

Wolf control in the Yukon again became controversial in 1992. Members of government agencies stating a need to protect the declining caribou herds, such as the Aishihik herd, have shot wolves from helicopters despite widespread protests.

ABOVE: Wolves need plenty of water, particularly after a big meal. Den and rendezvous sites are chosen in part because of their proximity to fresh water. **OPPOSITE:** The wolf was once the most widely distributed land mammal in the world. Wolves once lived throughout North America, Europe, and Asia but have vanished from most of their former range, except for a few scattered wilderness areas. If wolves are a symbol of the wild, then we must become aware of the tenuous existence of all creatures wild and wonderful.

Conservation organizations such as the Canadian Nature Federation and World Wildlife Fund Canada opposed the kills as biologically unjustified and expressed concerns that wolves within Kluane National Park would be killed as they traveled through territories that crossed over the park's protective boundaries.

Among the most secure areas for wolves in Canada, as in most of the world, are national parks. In 1990 World Wildlife Fund Canada outlined a Conservation Strategy for Large Carnivores in Canada to increase their protection within nature preserves by preserving and protecting habitats where carnivores would have the least impact from human populations.

Canada, the world's second largest country, devotes 2 percent of its land base to thirty-six national parks. Wolf populations can be found in at least half of those parks. Wolves are protected in one way or another within areas totaling approximately 2.5 percent of Canada's total land mass (or nearly eighty-five thousand square miles [220,150 sq km]).

Among the areas where wolf populations currently reside are Chapleau and Nipissing Crown Game Preserves and Algonquin and Lake Superior Provincial Parks in Ontario; Banff and Jasper National Parks in Alberta; Bowron Lakes Provincial Park, Strathcone Nature Conservancy Area, and Yoho-Kootenay National Park in British Columbia; La Maurice National Park in Quebec; Prince Albert National Park in Saskatchewan; and Riding Mountain National Park in Manitoba.

Canadian wolves, of course, do not recognize the border lines on human maps that delineate protected national park lands from potential danger zones. Neither do they recognize international boundaries such as those between Canada and the United States. Canadian wolves have been known to travel into the United States to recolonize areas of historic wolf habitat.

Northeastern United States

The area around Glacier National Park in Montana is a key area for wolf populations. Wolves are also returning to Wisconsin and Michigan, and there is a strong population in Minnesota.

The wolf presence in Minnesota is so strong, in fact, that in 1978 the wolf was downlisted and reclassified from endangered to threatened. Minnesota's estimated one thousand to twelve hundred wolves have a healthy population of white-tailed deer on which to feed. Even at the average of eighteen to twenty deer per wolf per year (two-thirds of which are fawns), wolves do not kill even half the number of deer registered annually by deer hunters in wolf range.

Healthy deer populations with a lack of predators have become problem deer populations in many parts of the eastern United States . Severe overpopulation—as high as 500,000 on the upper peninsula of Michigan—has resulted in large numbers of deaths from starvation.

In 1978, the United States Fish and Wildlife Service approved a recovery plan for the eastern timber wolf and revised it in 1992. The plan's goals include at least two viable populations of eastern timber wolves in the lower forty-eight states. While the Minnesota population has not only met but exceeded population goals, a second population outside Minnesota on Isle Royale, Michigan, must meet specific goals of its own.

If the wolves moving into the United States from Canada establish themselves within one hundred miles (161km) of the Minnesota wolves, then their ultimate population in late winter must reach one hundred. This number of wolves—before the pups are born in spring—will be considered a healthy, viable population. That number rises to two hundred if the new wolves are located more than one hundred miles from the Minnesota population.

OPPOSITE: Wolves can travel great distances over land, along rocky terrains, and even through shallow water. Wolves are, in fact, excellent swimmers.

This map shows states within the contiguous United States that have developed plans for reintroducing wolves.

FIVE POTENTIAL WOLF REIN-TRODUCTION SITES HAVE BEEN IDENTIFIED IN THE NORTHEAST:

1) Eastern Maine
2) Northwest Maine and adjacent portions of New Hampshire
3) New York's Adirondack Forest Preserve Area
4) Michigan's upper peninsula (a small wolf population already exists there)
5) Northern Wisconsin (a small wolf population already exists there)

Wolves from Minnesota apparently began reestablishing in Wisconsin soon after federal protection of wolves took effect in 1974. With a goal of at least eighty wolves, a recovery plan was established for Wisconsin between 1985 and 1989. Population statistics have fluctuated as Wisconsin's wolves have battled diseases ranging from parvovirus to Lyme disease and from heartworm to mange.

Not all the wolves that left northern Minnesota stopped in Wisconsin. Some continued on to the Upper Peninsula of Michigan. In the late 1980s, a pair of wolves was discovered in the central portion of the Upper Peninsula. This pair produced its first pups in the spring of 1991. After nearly three decades without wolves, the rugged forest lands that cover more than sixteen thousand square miles (41,440 sq km) of Michigan's Upper Peninsula provide abundant prey and abundant hopes for the wolf's survival.

Just as excitement began to peak at the return of the eastern timber wolf to these areas, concern was growing over the wolves on Isle Royale. Their history on this 210-square-mile (544 sq km) island national park is a fascinating one. During the extreme cold snap of the winter of 1949, an ice bridge formed, connecting Isle Royale to mainland Ontario, Canada, just fifteen miles (24km) away. Whether a whole pack or only a breeding pair of Canadian wolves traversed that bridge is not certain. But cross they did, and wolf numbers climbed.

Wildlife biologist L. David Mech began studying both the wolves and their relationship to the moose populations of Isle Royale in 1958. Early on, wolf and moose populations appeared to fluctuate in tandem. During the 1970s, however, the wolf population doubled from a single pack of twenty to twenty-five animals, eventually dividing into three packs with a total of fifty wolves on the island.

Suddenly, during the 1980s, the wolf population suffered a dramatic crash that did not correspond to the levels that would be expected from previous patterns based on prey availability. At one point, wolf numbers dropped as low as twelve animals, while prey numbers continued to increase. Finally, in 1992, the Isle Royale wolves produced pups. Their population started to grow again.

Researchers continue to follow the fluctuations of the wolf and prey populations to gain some insight into the causes and cycle patterns. While predator and prey populations do sometimes fluctuate wildly in response to extreme weather changes, there may be other factors contributing to the dramatic shifts on Isle Royale.

Some researchers suggest that, while moose are extremely abundant on the island, they are predominantly prime, healthy animals that are not easy prey for wolves. Thus, even in the midst of numerous moose, wolves go hungry and their populations crash. Others theorize that diseases such as parvovirus may be a factor—particularly for high wolf pup mortality. Or, because of their history of origin—frozen on the island after their ice bridge receded—Isle Royale's wolves, it is feared, may be suffering difficulties from heavy inbreeding.

The future may reveal fascinating glimpses into the ways small natural populations either adapt to these pressures or ultimately lose the fight for survival.

Glacier National Park

Like the Isle Royale wolves, the wolves in Glacier National Park got their start in Canada. In 1973, the same year Congress passed the Endangered Species Act, Montana passed its own law protecting wolves. Though wolves were sighted occasionally around that time in Glacier National Park, they were single wolves believed to be dispersing southward from Canadian wolf packs.

Then, in 1982, in 1984, and again in 1985, a breeding pair of wolves produced a litter near Glacier in British Columbia. The pack of twelve, which became known as the Magic Pack, migrated south into Glacier National Park in November 1985. As the breeding season approached, the alpha female selected a den site in the park and, in the spring of 1986, gave birth to five pups—the first in the park and in the western United States in decades.

Alaska

Alaska is home to the largest population of wolves in the United States. With an estimated six thousand to seven thousand wolves, Alaska's populations are not listed as endangered or threatened, as they are in the lower forty-eight states.

It is in Alaska that Adolph Murie did his intensive and acclaimed research on the East Fork Pack—research that changed the way many people, particularly some government wildlife managers, saw wolves.

Unfortunately, wildlife managers in Alaska thirty years after the publication of Murie's work bowed to hunting pressures. Some biologists became convinced that moose and caribou declines could be attributed predominantly to the growth of wolf populations. Between 1976 and 1982, the Alaska Department of Fish and Game began shooting more than 70 percent of the wolves in certain areas of Alaska, using helicopters to chase them down. Moose populations did increase in some areas following these control efforts, but some biologists point out that this could easily be attributed to natural population fluctuations that vary with weather patterns and availability of food.

What about the caribou? In 1987, the Alaska Board of Game determined that there had been no significant subsistence use of the Delta caribou herd (the herd population on which much of the wolf control has been based). The herd is hunted primarily for sport.

The government is not the only factor in wolf control. In the 1980s, about a thousand wolves per year were trapped and shot for skins or sport. There was no limit on the number of wolves a hunter could kill until 1989, and until 1991 land-and-shoot hunting was a common practice in Alaska. In this practice, hunters used airplanes to track wolves, then landed and left the plane to shoot from the ground. Abuse of these principles was significant. Wolves were shot from the airplanes or chased through open areas with little cover until, terrified and exhausted, they were easy targets from taxiing aircraft. Several accounts of such violations of not only the state regulations but the Federal Airborne Hunting Act were highly publicized. Many questioned the "sport" in such actions.

In actuality, dry summers, hard winters, human hunting pressures, natural migrations, and predators undoubtedly all played a role in the fluctuating levels of caribou and moose populations that game officials recorded in the late 1980s and early 1990s. The Alaska Board of Game's response, however, was distasteful to many and, for some, was shocking. In November 1992, the board approved a five-year aerial wolf control program designed to kill up to 80 percent of the wolves in three game-management areas northeast of Anchorage. Wolves would be fitted with radio collars and hunted from helicopters and airplanes.

For those in Alaska and the lower forty-eight states who opposed these measures, the attitude that wolves should be killed to allow more hunting opportunities for humans made little sense. They became further aggravated and frustrated by attitudes expressed by Alaska's governor, Walter Hickel, who responded to their concerns by saying, "You can't just let nature run wild."

More than two hundred national and international conservation organizations rallied to call for an international tourist boycott of Alaska. Faced with this potential threat to Alaska's one-billion-dollar tourist industry, Governor Hickel (who himself owned one of the largest hotels in Anchorage) suspended the aerial wolf control plan—at least briefly, and called for an international "Wolf Summit."

Would it be truly possible to reach an acceptable compromise between groups as diverse as state officials, wildlife biologists, environmentalists, hunters, and trappers? Many Alaskans claim it is their right to manage Alaska's wildlife resources their way—without interference from Americans in the lower forty-eight states. And many biologists contend that the proposed plan for wolf control was based on inaccurate or faulty biological premises and that wolf control would not greatly affect the caribou herd fluctuations.

OPPOSITE: White wolves are most often seen in the far north. But even in northern areas that are covered by snow and ice for most of the year, there are wolves of other coat colors as well.

The Delta caribou herd has varied widely in number, from a low of two thousand in 1976 to more than ten thousand (in the presence of wolves). There are many factors that relate to the Delta herd's recent decline, including harsh winters, summer droughts, and depressed reproduction, yet the herd is still at or near its average of the past fifty years, which is between three thousand and five thousand animals. The statewide caribou population more than tripled over the past fifteen years, and continues to increase. The debates at the Wolf Summit over the biological basis for wolf control were many. Within months of the Wolf Summit, another meeting of the Alaska Board of Game was set to discuss proposals.

These ninety-two proposals were submitted by conservationists, environmentalists, government agencies, hunters, trappers, wolf haters, and wolf lovers. At the board's discretion, some were reviewed, some tabled, some ignored.

The first proposals approved allowed aircraft-assisted, same-day airborne trapping of wolves using steel traps, snares, and even high-powered rifles. While the board stipulated that trappers be at least one hundred yards (91.5m) from their aircraft, state enforcement officials indicated that this regulation would be virtually impossible to enforce. Extended trapping seasons were approved to allow trappers improved weather conditions and longer periods of daylight.

The state's official wolf control plans, because of the close proximity of the areas to Denali National Park, would pose a serious threat to packs traveling

ABOVE: Wolves have served as convenient scapegoats for those who complain that herds of caribou, moose, and deer have been decimated by wolf predation, leaving too few animals for hunters to shoot. In fact, there is little evidence that suggests that wolves have a negative effect on the long-term health and survival of ungulate populations.

in and out of the park. The board, however, voted down proposals to extend and establish buffer zone areas adjacent to the borders of Denali National Park. The governor's office was inundated with calls and letters from both within and outside Alaska, indicating that public opinion was overwhelmingly against the state's proposals.

Should Alaska listen to opinions outside its own state? Alaska's game managers set wildlife management policies not only for the state lands, but for Alaska's millions of acres of federal lands. Alaska is charged with the responsibility of holding these natural resources in trust for all Americans.

During the 1993–1994 hunting and trapping season, nearly fifteen hundred wolves were legally killed in Alaska—the highest number in at least seventeen years, and a 40 percent increase over the previous season.

The year 1994 saw continued upheaval over wolf control in Alaska. In late November, Dr. Gordon Haber, a wildlife biologist who has studied Alaska's wolves and other wildlife for thirty years, had flown by helicopter to one of the Alaska Department of Fish and Game's wolf snaring stations. Video footage of what was found was broadcast over television in the state and was later picked up by media around the country.

Four wolves had been caught in snares, and three were still alive. One had chewed off its leg below the elbow in a desperate attempt to free itself. State laws restricted Haber from "interfering" with the wolves himself, so he radioed the pilot of an Alaska Department of Fish and Game airplane to send help. Further video footage showed a state wildlife official shooting a snared wolf five times before it died.

Two days later, the wolf control program was suspended and state personnel were instructed to remove nearly seven hundred snares from a one-thousand-square-mile (2,590 sq km) area in the Alaskan Range. Bald eagles, snow geese, and moose were among the other animals caught in the traps intended for wolves.

Despite continued public outrage, in the spring of 1995 the Alaskan legislature was considering Senate Bill 81 to create "harvest incentive areas" and pay private hunters and trappers a bounty of two hundred dollars for each wolf killed within these areas. During the final week of March, the Alaska Board of Game approved wolf and bear control over areas stretching tens of thousands of square miles. This was in response to an "intensive game management law" (SB77) passed in 1994.

What will be the fate of Alaska's wolves as a new century approaches? The wolves deserve better stewardship than we have provided in the past.

This story was told by wildlife author Brenda Peterson on her return from the Wolf Summit in a *Seattle Times* article of January 27, 1993, titled "We Must Control Ourselves, Not Wolves." It may be an indication of the work that lies ahead if the wolf is to have a fighting chance in Alaska.

On the last day of the wolf summit I sat in a bar and listened to someone tell a story of his father, an Alaskan trapper. "The wolf is so much like our species, " the man said. "They have families, a social structure that's complex and highly organized. They're top predators who even kill their own kind, although never like our human wars. They are our mirrors. Maybe that's why we've killed so many of them, just like we've killed our own kind. But the wolf and us, we recognize each other."

Then he told the story: Seems his trapper father came back to his trap lines and found a fierce wolf, his paw clamped shut and broken in the metal trap. "He just looked at me, that old wolf," the man said. "Maybe he thought after suffering like that for days that I was going to help him. Don't know why, but that creature stared at me and wagged his tail. He wagged his tail like that, until I shot him."

Yellowstone

Recently, public attitudes about and focus on wolves have perhaps been felt most keenly in Yellowstone National Park. Following a federal eradication program that began in 1870, wolves were almost completely absent from the park—the last year more than a single wolf was seen in Yellowstone was 1926.

The 2.2-million-acre (880,000 ha) park was established by Congress on March 1, 1872, "...as a public park or pleasuring ground for the benefit and enjoyment of the people." Apparently, wolves did not fit into these objectives, though they were a part of the park's native fauna. Like so many areas in the 1800s, Yellowstone National Park was checkered with the strychnine-studded trails of the wolfers. Carcasses laced with poison were effective bait for wolves.

But it was Park Service Rangers, not wolfers, who, in 1923, destroyed Yellowstone's last known wolf den.

Three years later, the last wolf was gone from Yellowstone National Park.

It would be nearly fifty years before the signing of the Endangered Species Act required the restoration of species in danger of extinction either in a specific region or throughout an entire range. In 1975, the Northern Rocky Mountain wolf was listed as endangered. The first recovery plan for the wolf was completed in 1977, but no specific recommendation for reintroducing wolves to Yellowstone was made in that plan.

By 1980, however, a wolf recovery plan recommending that wolves be reintroduced to Yellowstone was signed, though no action was ever taken. It would be seven more years before a revised plan would be signed; this plan prompted a bill calling for wolf reintroduction to be proposed by Utah Representative Wayne Owens. The 1987 Recovery Plan set a goal of establishing at least three wolf populations of about a hundred wolves each.

ABOVE: The majority of residents in the northwestern United States support wolf reintroduction efforts. In Yellowstone National Park, wolf recovery makes sound ecological sense. **OPPOSITE:** Yellowstone is home to a wide variety of animal and plant species, and with wolf packs roaming the park's land it is once again a complete ecosystem.

Between 1987 and 1988, attempts to initiate the necessary Environmental Impact Statement were thwarted by reintroduction opponents in the Senate. In an effort to alleviate the fears on which much of the opposition to wolf reintroduction was based, Defenders of Wildlife began raising more than $100,000 to establish a fund to reimburse ranchers for any livestock losses that could be attributed to wolves.

At the same time, a study of the area, conducted by the Department of the Interior, was launched. Released in May 1990, the six-hundred-page report titled "Wolves for Yellowstone?" pointed out that it would be possible to restore wolves with minimal impact not only on livestock and local economies, but on other wildlife as well. The study reported that wolf recovery and reintroduction in the park made sound ecological sense.

Finally, in the autumn of 1991, Congress authorized and directed the United States Fish and Wildlife Service to prepare a draft Environmental Impact Statement on wolf reintroduction in Yellowstone National Park and central Idaho. Part of this process included a series of public hearings and opportunities for comment on the plans.

A follow-up study to the earlier "Wolves for Yellowstone?" report was released in July 1992, and reported that public support for a Yellowstone wolf reintroduction was strong and that wolf recovery would benefit the region. Then, on September 30, 1992, a hunter shot and killed a wolf just south of Yellowstone—a wolf believed to have traveled from northwestern Montana.

Defenders of Wildlife, again in an effort to provide incentives for local residents to support wolves, established a program to award landowners five thousand dollars when wolves successfully rear a litter of pups on their property.

The pros and cons of wolf recovery were debated extensively in 1993 when the draft Environmental Impact Statement was released. It included proposals for reintroducing wolves to Yellowstone National Park and central Idaho if naturally occurring packs were not found in either region prior to October 1994.

Five alternatives were proposed in the draft Environmental Impact Statement:

Alternative 1—Reintroduction of Experimental Populations Alternative (U.S. Fish and Wildlife Proposal)

Alternative 2—Natural Recovery Alternative (No Action Alternative—Encourage wolf populations to naturally expand into Idaho and Yellowstone)

Alternative 3—No Wolves Alternative (Change laws to prevent wolf recovery)

Alternative 4—Wolf Management Committee Alternative (Establish legislation allowing states to implement wolf recovery and management without federal oversight or intervention)

Alternative 5—Reintroduction of Nonexperimental Wolves Alternative (Reintroduction with strong protection for wolves without creating an experimental population rule)

The draft Environmental Impact Statement recommended that wolves be reintroduced to Yellowstone and central Idaho under the experimental population provision of the Endangered Species Act. The public was invited to comment on the draft Environmental Impact Statement between July 1 and November 26, 1993—and comment they did. More than 160,000 individuals, organizations, and government agencies commented via letters, resolutions, testimony at public hearings, and signed petitions. This incredible response was a record for a federal Environmental Impact

Statement. Of the responses, 100,000 were in favor of the recovery program.

Once all the public comments were analyzed, a final Environmental Impact Statement was completed on May 4, 1994, recommending wolf reintroduction in Yellowstone and central Idaho. It was sent to decision makers in the United States Fish and Wildlife Service and the Department of the Interior to determine how wolf recovery would proceed.

On June 14th, immediately following a mandatory thirty-day waiting period, Secretary of the Interior Bruce Babbitt signed the Record of Decision on the Environmental Impact Statement, approving the United States Fish and Wildlife Service recommendations. Wolves would be reintroduced using the "experimental nonessential population" provision of the Endangered Species Act. This provision allows management of wolves by both government agencies and the public in order to minimize conflicts over wolf depredation on livestock.

The Interior Department's final version of rules governing the reintroduction plans included several changes from the draft version. Most significant was a stipulation for a full review of the reintroduction within three years. Other changes allowed for greater flexi-

ABOVE: Wolf predation on livestock does sometimes occur but, according to the U.S. Fish and Wildlife Service, it is unusual enough to be considered aberrant. Wolves are most likely to kill cattle and sheep in summer, when herds are let loose to graze on open grassland.

bility for private citizens to harass wolves or even kill wolves caught attacking livestock.

If all went as planned, reintroduction would result in wolf population recovery (ten breeding pairs of about a hundred wolves for three successive years) in Yellowstone and central Idaho by the year 2002.

On November 25, 1994, at just about the time wolves were supposed to be transported from Canada to acclimatization pens in Yellowstone, a lawsuit aimed at stopping the reintroduction was filed. The American Farm Bureau Association, in conjunction with the state Farm Bureaus of Wyoming, Montana, and Idaho, filed suit in Federal District Court in Wyoming, claiming that the government didn't sufficiently analyze the potential impact of wolf reintroduction on ranchers, wildlife, and public land use. With the preliminary injunction hearing set for December 21, the United States Fish and Wildlife Service agreed to delay the transfer of wolves from Canada until January 1, 1995.

The Sierra Club Legal Defense Fund then gave notice of its intent to file a lawsuit, arguing that the wolves in Idaho wouldn't have adequate protection under the "experimental nonessential" designation. Wolves already in Idaho would lose the protection they had already gained as an endangered species.

Just before Christmas, the Farm Bureau requested a preliminary injunction against the Yellowstone reintroduction and was heard in United States District Court. On January 3, 1995, the request was denied.

In the mountains of Alberta, Canada, the first of thirty wolves was captured, tagged with a radio collar, crated, and readied for a trip by air and truck to either Yellowstone National Park or central Idaho. On January 11, shipping began.

At the same time, the Wyoming Farm Bureau filed an emergency appeal in Denver, Colorado, in the Tenth Circuit Court of Appeals to bar release of the wolves. A forty-eight-hour stay was granted.

While the court reviewed the case, the wolves waited in their crates. The stay was lifted early, but the wolves had been in the cramped crates for more than thirty-six hours before their release into special acclimation pens in Yellowstone.

Two days later, on January 14, four wolves who had been held back in an airplane hanger ran free in Idaho's Frank Church-River of No Return Wilderness Area. Within a week, eleven more wolves from Canada were released in Idaho.

All the wolves were fitted with radio collars so that they could be monitored from the air. Shortly after release, one was killed by a farmer who claimed that the wolf had killed a calf. The wolf may have been feeding on the animal, but veterinary pathologists at the United States Fish and Wildlife Service forensic lab in Oregon who examined the calf determined it had died of "complications associated with birth." It was definately not killed by the wolf.

The remaining Idaho wolves have traveled extensively within an area of about ten thousand square miles, (25,000 sq km) including central and eastern Idaho and parts of western Montana.

In Yellowstone, on January 20, an additional six wolves joined the group released into the one-acre (0.4ha) enclosures. There they would live until March 21, 1995, when they would be free to choose territories for themselves from Yellowstone's 2.2 million acres (880,000ha) and to hunt the park's wild populations of elk, mule deer, moose, white-tailed deer, bison, pronghorn antelope, bighorn sheep, and mountain goats.

With the wolf established in Yellowstone National Park, the largest ecosystem in the lower forty-eight states was once again complete.

By the late 1980s, four packs were identified in or near the park. Within Glacier National Park reside the North Camas Pack and the South Camas Pack. The territory of the Spruce Creek Pack spans an area that includes part of Glacier National Park and extends north into British Columbia. The Headwaters Pack, while within twenty miles of Glacier National Park, makes its territory in Canada.

Wolves traveling from Canada into the United States have been making headlines now for years, most recently with the move of wolves from Canada to Yellowstone National Park (with a little help from their friends, this time).

South of the United States border, however, there is also news of wolves.

THE MEXICAN WOLF

The plan produced by the Mexican Wolf Recovery Team was signed by U.S. and Mexican officials in 1982. The efforts to save this critically endangered subspecies of the gray wolf are truly international in scope. The recovery team includes representatives from both countries, and the breeding population is maintained by organizations in both countries. In addition, attempts to determine whether any Mexican wolves are still alive in Mexico are joint Mexico/United States projects. Under the direction of Dr. Julio Carrera several organizations—including Proteccion de la Fauna Mexican A.C., the Mexican government, the United States Fish and Wildlife Service, the National Fish and Wildlife Foundation, Arizona Fish and Game, and Wolf Haven International—have assisted in field surveys in Mexico by providing training, staff, equipment, and funding. Traveling hundreds of square miles predominantly in the Sierra Madre Range, people trained to howl like wolves call out in the night and document responses using sensitive sound-recording equipment.

Recovery efforts in the United States are focused on breeding wolves and determining appropriate sites for their future reintroduction. The two most likely sites are:

1) The White Sands Missile Range—a four-thousand-square-mile (10,360 sq km) site in southern New Mexico. This mountainous environment covered with desert shrub is home to nearly eight thousand white-tailed deer, thousands of wild horses, and gemsbok, as well as healthy populations of cougars and coyotes. Cattle have not been allowed in the area for more than fifty years.

2) The Blue Range area—a seven-thousand-square-mile (18,130 sq km) area within the Apache and Gile Nation Forests of eastern Arizona and western New Mexico. Pinon, juniper, and evergreen oak trees make up this extensive forest area that supports more than seventy thousand mule deer, white-tailed deer, and elk, as well as several thousand javelina, pronghorn, and bighorn sheep. Cattle do graze throughout the area. Predators include black bear, bobcats, cougars, coyotes, and foxes.

Opposition to the recovery plans came as early as 1987, when the military, worried about unhappy neighbors and the difficulties of reintroducing wolves to the White Sands site, nearly shut the program down. Regional support was so strong, however, that groups devoted to the plan quickly sprang into action. In New Mexico, the Mexican Wolf Coalition was formed. Preserve Arizona's Wolves (PAWS) began in Arizona, and the Mexican Wolf Coalition of Texas joined in. Pointing to the requirements of the Endangered Species Act, they stood up for the Mexican wolf, and the recovery program continued.

The concerns of proponents and opponents are heard and addressed in the process of developing the Environmental Impact Statement. Ranchers fear not only for their livestock, but for the land-use restrictions they feel will be imposed as wolves are reintroduced. They worry particularly about whether or not they will be allowed to continue grazing their cattle on federal lands—lands the ranchers have traditionally been allowed to lease for this purpose.

A new concern is also being expressed from some who feel that reintroducing wolves is cruel. Fearing that the historical persecution of wolves will also return, some people are opposed to recovery efforts.

For the rancher who fears loss of livestock, Defenders of Wildlife has set up a $100,000 livestock compensation fund. Concerted education efforts are perhaps the best hope of addressing the fears that reintroduced wolves will face the same persecution as their historical counterparts. The fact that there is great public support for the recovery efforts is a good indication of changing philosophies.

THE RED WOLF

Declared an endangered species in 1967, the red wolf's relationship with humans through history is not too dissimilar to the gray wolf's. The red wolf, *Canis rufus*, once ranged through much of the southeastern United States, from Texas to Florida.

Habitat destruction and persecution were key in the demise of the red wolf, but an interesting relationship with another member of the canid family also plays a part in the red wolf's history. Adaptable to an extreme, coyotes have filled many of the niches left void as gray wolf populations were destroyed. So, too, did coyotes establish themselves in former red wolf territory as these less adaptable wolves declined in number and wilderness areas were plowed for farmland or zoned for cities.

Some biologists believe that red wolves, with their population so depressed, began to interbreed with coyotes, gradually blurring the species lines. Other researchers question whether hybridization might not have always taken place between the red wolf and the coyote, or even that the red wolf is actually a gray wolf/coyote hybrid. As the thoughts of a red wolf recovery program took form, the hybrid issue was not dismissed: it would continue to rise and fall throughout the life of the program.

An initial red wolf recovery plan was established, and the first red wolf, a female, arrived at the Point Defiance Zoo and Aquarium in Tacoma, Washington in 1969. It would be another year before a male would join her to make the breeding program viable. In the meantime, the wild red wolf population continued to decline as the species' range was reduced to small coastal areas in Texas and Louisiana.

The captive population, holding at one male and two females, faltered as the Endangered Species Act became law. By 1974 the threat of extinction loomed so large that full-force efforts to collect wild red wolves for captive breeding began. At the end of 1976, the captive population stood at eight males and nine females, all wild wolves captured for the breeding program. In 1977 the first litters of red wolves was born in captivity. The total captive count: eighteen males and seventeen females.

Efforts to reintroduce red wolves into the wild posed problems as well. In 1976, at least one of a pair of red wolves released on five-thousand-acre (2,000ha) Bull's Island, located off the coast of South Carolina, decided not to stay on the island. The wolf traveled three miles (5km) through marshland to reach the mainland. Between January and November 1978, the first successful experimental release, tracking, and recapture of red wolves was completed on Bull's Island. This time the pair was housed in an enclosure for six months to acclimatize them to their new surroundings. Their stay—once the wolves were released—lasted eight months, and there were no problems encountered.

The last pure red wolves from the wild were brought into the captive-breeding program in 1979, and the following year, the red wolf was declared extinct in the wild. The breeding program's success, however, with population numbers increasing annually, allowed other organizations to join the effort.

An important step toward reintroduction came in 1984 with the establishment of the Alligator River National Wildlife Refuge on 118,000 acres (47,200 ha) of donated land along the northeastern coast of North Carolina. Two years later, four pairs of red wolves arrived at the reserve—the key focus of the nation's first reintroduction program in the United States. The first pair was released into the wild on September 14, 1987. On April 28, 1988, the first litter of pups was born in the wild at Alligator River National Wildlife Reserve.

Additional release sites would herald the continued success of the program:

1989—Horn Island off the coast of Mississippi

1990—Saint Vincent's Island, Florida, and Durante Island, North Carolina

1991—The 500,000-acre (200,00) Great Smokey Mountains National Park, located in Tennessee along the mountainous border with North Carolina

In 1992, a study on the genetic makeup of the red wolf failed to determine any consistent genetic differ-

As a debate over its status as a distinct wolf species or subspecies rages, the red wolf teeters on the brink of extinction. A determination that the red wolf is actually a coyote/gray wolf hybrid could have a significant impact on red wolf conservation and reintroduction efforts.

ences between the red wolves being released in North Carolina and coyote/gray wolf hybrids. The ongoing debate over the status of the red wolf escalated, and within weeks of the publication of these findings, ranchers in Tennessee and North Carolina petitioned the United States Fish and Wildlife Service to remove the red wolf from the Endangered Species List. The ramifications would have been enormous for the red wolf. Even the two American scientists who published these scientific findings felt that misinterpretation based on preliminary information was a possibility, and urged that no firm conclusions be drawn too quickly. Any conclusion that the red wolf is not a separate species or subspecies could result in the loss of legal protection for the animal under the Endangered Species Act.

The final determination has not been made regarding the red wolf's genetic origin. All the animals in the Red Wolf Recovery Program today are the progeny of the fourteen pure red wolves taken into captivity years ago. The goal of the captive breeding program is to have 330 wolves in captivity and 220 at three mainland reintroduction sites. Each reintroduction area has a population goal as well.

Between 1987 and 1993, fifty-seven captive-born red wolves were released at the Alligator River National Wildlife Refuge, and at least thirty-nine wolves were born in the wild. Interestingly, survival of the wild-born wolves has been significantly greater than that of the captive-born animals released in this area.

The reintroduction has shown such great progress in the Alligator River National Wildlife Refuge that another refuge was added to the program in 1993. In August and September of that year, two red wolf family groups were released at the Pocosin Lake National Wildlife Refuge in northeastern North Carolina.

The first project to restore to its former range a species that was declared extinct in the wild has been a great success. Future projects can learn an enormous amount from the Red Wolf Recovery Program. Preserving suitable habitat is crucial. Also vital to survival is the assurance that there are sufficient numbers of animals reintroduced; these populations must be able to handle a variety of obstacles such as diseases and competition with other species. In order to have strong enough populations to survive on their own, the red wolves in North Carolina needed five years and the supplemental release of about forty-five wolves.

Now those wolves are faced with a new challenge. On July 1, 1994, the North Carolina General Assembly ratified a bill entitled "An Act to Allow the Trapping and Killing of Red Wolves by Owners of Private Land." According to the Red Wolf Newsletter, Volume 7, Number 1, Summer/Fall 1994:

> Ratification of the act was based on the opinion that red wolves in Hyde and Washington counties endanger livestock, wildlife and people. Since 1987, 15 incidents have been reported, seven involving wolves. These seven incidents have prompted the Fish and Wildlife Service (Service) to return wolves to captivity or translocate them to new areas....The topic of wolf interactions with livestock, wildlife and people generated much emotion in the region. However, this issue probably had less influence on ratification of the act than the belief of local citizens that the wolf project was causing them to once again abdicate their rights to the Federal government. Since 1984 the Service has maintained that implementing a successful wolf reintroduction program requires involvement of local citizens in the decision-making process. Throughout August 1992 the Service hosted a series of meetings with commissioners from Hyde, Tyrell, Dare, Washington, and Beaufort counties and residents of those communities. People attending the meetings stated that landowners should have nearly complete control over wolves on their property, a position the Service agrees with. Indeed, comments received at the public meetings prompted the Service to develop new regulations governing the wolf program which are now being finalized.

> It has been said that wolves present the greatest test of human wisdom and good intentions. If so, residents of northeastern North Carolina have passed with flying colors; the red wolf reintroduction effort has been successful largely because local citizens have been good stewards of the wolf population....We are now ushering in a phase of wolf recovery that will provide local citizens unprecedented control over the fate of an endangered species. Clearly the red wolf program will continue to test the wisdom and intentions of local citizens as well as the nation.

Threatened, Endangered, Extinct...

Given the wolf's troubled history, it is not surprising that this fascinating animal is long gone from much of its former range.

Species labeled as threatened by the Endangered Species Act are those with greatly depleted numbers. They are seen as likely to be classified as endangered in all or a significant area of their range in the foreseeable future.

An endangered species is one in immediate danger of extinction throughout all or in a significant area of its range. The continued survival of an endangered species is precarious because of factors such as habitat destruction, disease, or exploitation.

A species is classified as extinct once it has ceased to exist entirely. A species is sometimes referred to as "extinct in the wild," which means that it no longer exists in its natural habitat, but that animals still live in captivity; there is some hope for these species because captive populations, once stable, may be reintroduced into the wild. True extinction for any animal—like the dodo, the Carolina parakeet, and Stellar's sea cow—really does mean forever. More than five and possibly as many as eleven formerly recognized species or subspecies of wolf are now extinct.

Many wolf populations in the United States—in fact, all but those in Alaska and Minnesota—are considered endangered. Throughout the world, in those areas where healthy wolf populations do exist (such as Alaska, Canada, and Russia), conservationists have tried to work together to develop accepted standards for the management of wolves. These standards were formally documented as a Manifesto on Wolf Conservation by the International Union for the Conservation of Nature (IUCN) and Natural Resources Wolf Specialist Group in September 1973, which was updated in January 1983 and reprinted in January 1993.

The standards, while in no way legally binding, are widely accepted and include a Declaration of Principles for Wolf Conservation together with recommended Guidelines for Wolf Conservation.

DECLARATION OF PRINCIPLES FOR WOLF CONSERVATION

1. Wolves, like all other wildlife, have a right to exist in a wild state. This right is in no way related to their known value to mankind. Instead, it derives from the right of all living creatures to coexist with man as part of the natural ecosystems.

2. The wolf pack is a highly developed and unique social organization. The wolf is one of the most adaptable and important mammalian predators. It has one of the widest natural geographical distributions of any mammal. It has been, and in some cases still is, the most important predator of big-game animals in the Northern Hemisphere. In this role, it has undoubtedly played an important part in the evolution of such species and, in particular, of those characteristics which have made many of them desirable game animals.

3. It is recognized that wolf populations have differentiated into subspecies which are genetically adapted to particular environments. It is of first importance that these local populations be maintained in their natural environments in a wild state. Maintenance of genetic purity of locally adapted races is a responsibility of agencies which plan to reintroduce wolves into the wild as well as zoological gardens that may prove a source for such reintroductions.

4. Throughout recorded history man has regarded the wolf as undesirable and has sought to exterminate it. In more than half of the countries of the world where the wolf

existed, man has either succeeded, or is on the verge of succeeding, in exterminating the wolf.

5. This harsh judgment on the wolf has been based, first, on fear of the wolf as a predator of man and second, on hatred because of its predation on domestic livestock and on large wild animals. Historical perspectives suggest that to a consider-able extent the first fear has been based on myth rather than on fact. It is now evident that the wolf can no longer be considered a serious threat to man. It is true, however, that the wolf has been, and in some cases still is, a predator of some consequence on domestic livestock and wildlife.

6. The response of man, as reflected by the actions of individuals and governments,

ABOVE: Efforts for wolf conservation must be international in scope if we are to save seriously endangered wolf subspecies. This wolf, *Canis lupus arabs,* lives in the southern Negev Desert of Israel, and is highly threatened due to destruction of its natural habitat.

has been to try to exterminate the wolf. This is an unfortunate situation because the possibility now exists for the development of management programs which would mitigate serious problems, while at the same time permitting the wolf to live in many areas of the world where its presence would be acceptable.

7. It is recognized that occasionally there may be a scientifically established need to reduce nonendangered wolf populations; further it may become scientifically established that in certain endangered wolf populations specific individuals must be removed by appropriate conservation authorities for the benefit of wolf populations. Conflict with man sometimes occurs from undue economic competition or from imbalanced predator-prey ratios adversely affecting prey species and/or the wolf itself. In such cases, temporary reduction of wolf populations may become necessary, but reduction measures should be imposed under strict scientific management. The methods must be selective, be specific to the problem, be highly discriminatory, and have minimal adverse effects on the ecosystem. Alternative ecosystem management, including alteration of human activities and attitudes and nonlethal methods of wolf management, should be fully considered before lethal wolf reduction is employed. The goal of wolf management programs must be to restore and maintain a healthy balance in all components of the ecosystem. Wolf reduction should never result in the permanent extirpation of the species from any portion of its natural range.

8. The effect of major alterations of the environment through economic development may have serious consequences for the survival of wolves and their prey species in areas where wolves now exist. Recognition of the importance and status of wolves should be taken into account by legislation and in planning for the future of any region.

9. Scientific knowledge of the role of the wolf in ecosystems is inadequate in most countries in which the wolf still exists. Management should be established only on a firm scientific basis, having regard for international, national, and regional situations. However, existing knowledge is at least adequate to develop preliminary programs to conserve and manage the wolf throughout its range.

10. The maintenance of wolves in some areas may require that society at large bear the cost, e.g., by giving compensation for the loss of domestic stock; conversely there are areas having high agricultural value where it is not desirable to maintain wolves and where their introduction would not be feasible.

11. In some cases there has been a marked change in public attitudes toward the wolf. This change in attitudes has influenced governments to revise and even to eliminate archaic laws. It is recognized that education to establish a realistic picture of the wolf and its role in nature is most essential to wolf survival. Education programs, however, must be factual and accurate.

12. Socioeconomic, ecological, and political factors must be considered and resolved prior to reintroduction of the wolf into biologically suitable areas from which it has been extirpated.

The Endangered Species Act— in Danger

When a bitter fight over the Endangered Species Act raged in 1992, the debate was postponed by tacit agreement. It was an election year, and there was environmental controversy enough over the spotted owl in the Pacific Northwest.

The fight has been taken up again, and the Endangered Species Act is in great danger of being weakened. The controversy, according to opponents of the Endangered Species Act, stems from the view that it is uncompromising in its mission to save endangered species and is uncaring with regard to human and economic impacts. Proponents argue that extinction is a difficult thing on which to compromise. A species cannot, after all, be a little bit extinct.

The purpose of the Endangered Species Act has always been twofold:

1) To provide protection for animals in danger of extinction.

2) To create a means for recovery or restoration of species listed as threatened or endangered, taking into account the views of state and federal agencies, private organizations, and individuals who are affected by the process.

In 1978 a process was adopted in which a development project that could not be "reconciled" with an endangered species could be exempted from the requirements of the Endangered Species Act if it passed the review and approval of a high-level committee.

Congress amended the Endangered Species Act in 1982, adding a provision that allowed for the establishment of "experimental populations."

In 1995 the House of Representatives voted to suspend, at least temporarily, all new listings of endangered species. Senator Slade Gorton (R-WA) introduced legislation to "reform" the Endangered Species Act. Among other provisions, the bill requires the Secretary of the Interior to set a "conservation objective" for each species that may include but does not require recovery. The setting of these conservation objectives does not provide for public input. Obligations currently in place for federal agencies to consult with United States Fish and Wildlife Service and the National Marine Fisheries Service regarding potential impacts of federal actions on species survival would no longer be mandatory if this bill were passed.

In a frenzy to create a new bill, field hearings on the Endangered Species Act were rushed and incomplete. Committee markup of a new bill was scheduled for June 28, 1995. One month before the June deadline, House Speaker Newt Gingrich testified before the House Endangered Species Act Task Force, urging members to slow the process and plan a meeting to work out changes during the August recess.

At the same time, on May 25, a National Academy of Science panel released its report on the Endangered Species Act, urging Congress to strengthen the act. For years, Congress had directed the National Academy of Science to examine the "science behind the Endangered Species Act." Michael T. Glegg, Chairman of the Committee on Scientific Issues in the Endangered Species Act, said, "Our committee finds there has been a good match between science and the Endangered Species Act."

The report stresses not only the role the Endangered Species Act has played and can continue to play in preventing the extinction of some species and slowing the decline of others, but recommends further provisions to protect habitat:

> The ESA, in emphasizing habitat, reflects the current scientific understanding of the crucial biological role that habitat plays for species....Because habitat plays such an important biological role in endangered species survival, some core amount of essential habitat should be designated for protection at the time of listing a species as endangered as an emergency stop-gap measure.

The Endangered Species Act has been successful. Bald eagles have returned to skies from which they had disappeared. Countless lifesaving medicinal plants have been protected. Wolves once again fill their vital role in the Yellowstone ecosystem.

Wilderness areas are not luxuries. If the Endangered Species Act is in danger, so are we.

Voices We Shall Never Hear

Wolves are returning to lands they long ago roamed. They are returning on their own and with help from conservationists.

Ultimately, the wolves are returning because we are allowing them to return. Our relationship to wolves, and to other animals, is once again changing. We are beginning to recognize that it is not wolves or predators as a group that we need to control, but rather ourselves. The world's human population has more than doubled in the last fifty years, from 2.5 billion to 5.5 billion people. All of us place demands on natural resources.

We must acknowledge that limits on human expansion do exist, if we are to preserve the balance of nature. We must commit to a shift in values, from selective conservancy to a preservation of intact ecosystems. In *The Kingdom: Wildlife in North America*, Douglas Chadwick states:

> A fundamental issue revolves around wolves. Are we really out to conserve wilderness? Or only the pieces that suit us? To the extent that we pick and choose pieces, wildlife communities will reveal that much more about the temporary goals of human communities and that much less about the holistic workings of nature. How, then, shall we ever understand creation?

Other creatures should not require our justification to exist—it is inherent in their very being. Still, it is naive to think that the wolf can survive on its own; conservation efforts with a firm base of public support are the lifeblood of the wolf's continued existence. The same is true for many animals—the gorilla, the giant panda, the California condor, the blue whale, Przewalski's horse, the pygmy hippopotamus, the cheetah, the spotted owl, and countless others.

The greatest threat to wild animals is the destruction of their habitats through deforestation, agricultural practices, and the demands of an ever-increasing human population. The tools of farming and animal husbandry brought a new ease to the lives of humans, but they also brought a sense of alienation from wild animals.

Throughout history there have been those who challenged us to see that our own survival is tied to the preservation of nature as a whole. In the United States, the Endangered Species Act was among the first definitive steps in that direction. Today, national and international conservation programs embrace the preservation of wilderness as a cooperative effort. No single individual or organization can save a species or an ecosystem; whole nations must act in concert to preserve the legacies of the natural world before they disappear.

Wolves are returning home only because there is a home of sorts to which they can return. But what will become of animals in the future if their natural habitat is completely decimated? Are we willing to accept that they can never go home again?

Balancing the needs of a large and complex human society with the requirements of our animal neighbors is perhaps the greatest test of ingenuity before us today. Our success in meeting this single challenge will be the most important factor in the survival of the wolf and, indeed, of scores of other species—including our own.

ORGANIZATIONS

United States

Friends of the Wolf Sanctuary (FWS)
P.O. Box 760
Eureka, MO 63025
(314) 938-5900

Help Our Wolves Live (HOWL)
4600 Emerson Avenue South
Minneapolis, MN 55409
(612) 827-3402

Mexican Wolf Coalition of Texas (MWCT)
P.O. Box 1526
Spring, TX 77383
(713) 443-0012

Mission: Wolf
P.O. Box 211
Silver Cliff, CO 81249
(719) 746-2919

North American Wolf Society (NAWS)
P.O. Box 82950
Fairbanks, AK 99708
(907) 474-7355

Predator Project
P.O. Box 6733
Bozeman, MT 59771
(406) 587-3389

Preserve Arizona's Wolves
1413 East Dobbins Road
Phoenix, AZ 85040

Project Wolf U.S.A. (PWUSA)
168 Galer Street
Seattle, WA 98109
(206) 283-1957

Wild Canid Survival and Research Center
  (WCSRC)
P.O. Box 760
Eureka, MO 63025
(314) 938-5900

Wolf Fund
P.O. Box 471
Moose, WY 83012
(307) 733-0740

Wolf Haven International
3111 Offut Lake Road
Tenino, WA 98589
(206) 264-4695

Canada

Canadian Wolf Defenders
Box 3480 Station D
Edmonton, Alberta
Canada T5L 4JB

Friends of the Wolf
P.O. Box 21032 Glebe Postal Outlet
Ottawa, Ontario
Canada K1S 2H0

Northwest Wildlife Preservation Center
Box 34129 Station D
Vancouver, British Columbia
Canada V6J 4N3

Europe

Egholm Wolf Center
Egholmveg 42, DK-4880
Nysted, Denmark

European Wolf Network
Linderhof 2, 82488
Ettal, Germany

Foreningen Vare Rovdyr
Postboks 17, N-2420
Trysil, Norway

Foreningen Varggruppen
Box 15061, S-104
65 Stockholm, Sweden

Gesellschaft zum Schutz der Woelfe
Blassbacher Str. 55
6330 Wetzlar, 26 Germany

Grupo Lobo
Dept. de Zoologia e Antropologia
Faculdade de Ciancias, Bloco C-2
30 Piso Cidade Univ.
600 Lisbon, Portugal

Les Loups de Gevaudan
Sainte-Lucie 48100
Marjejois, France

Wolf Society of Great Britain
Moon Cottage, Kingswood Lane
Hindhead, Surrey
England GU26 6DQ

FURTHER READING

Alderton, David. *Foxes, Wolves, and Wild Dogs of the World*. New York: Facts on File, 1994.

Brandenburg, Jim. *Brother Wolf: A Forgotten Promise*. Minocqua, Wis.: NorthWord Press, 1993.

———. *White Wolf: Living with an Arctic Legend*. Minocqua, Wis.: NorthWood Press, 1990.

Busch, Robert. *The Wolf Almanac*. New York: Lyons and Burford, 1995.

Busch, Robert, ed. *Wolf Songs: The Classic Collection of Writings About Wolves*. San Francisco: Sierra Club Books, 1994.

Fischer, Hank. *Wolf Wars*. Billings, Mont.: 1995.

Fox, Michael W. *The Soul of the Wolf: A Meditation on Wolves and Man*. New York: Lyons and Burford, 1980.

Grooms, Steve. *The Return of the Wolf*. Minocqua, Wis.: NorthWood Press, 1993.

Link, Mike, and Kate Crowley. *Following the Pack: Leading Wolf Researchers*. Stillwater, Minn.: Voyageur Press, 1994.

Lopez, Barry H. *Of Wolves and Men*. New York: Simon & Schuster, 1979.

McIntyre, Rick. *A Society of Wolves: National Parks and the Battle Over the Wolf*. Stillwater, Minn.: Voyageur Press, 1993.

McIntyre, Rick, ed. *War Against the Wolf: America's Campaign to Exterminate the Wolf*. Stillwater, Minn.: Voyageur Press, 1995.

Mech, L. David. *Living with the Pack*. Stillwater, Minn.: Vogageur Press, 1988.

———. *The Way of the Wolf*. Stillwater, Minn.: Voyageur Press, 1991.

———. *The Wolf: The Ecology and Behavior of an Endangered Species*. University of Minnesota Press, 1981.

Murray, John A. *Out Among the Wolves: Contemporary Writings on the Wolf*. Alaska Northwest, 1993.

Savage, Candace. *Wolves*. San Francisco: Sierra Club Books, 1990.

Wolfe, Art. *In the Presence of Wolves*. New York: Crown, 1995.

PHOTOGRAPHY CREDITS

INDEX

Foxes
  Arctic, 41
  gray, 41–42
  red, 40–41

G
Gray wolves, 27, 32, *32*, *33*, 38, 54, 116–129
Greenland, 56

H
Hesperocyon, 26, *26*
Howling, 89, *89*, *90*, *91*
Hunting, 41
  collective, 52, 67
  by wolves, 29, 52, 67, 70–75
  of wolves, 17, 32, 104, 106–111, 122
Hybrids, 44, 46

I
Intelligence, 29, 52

J
Jackals, 39, *39*, 54

L
Lycaon pictus, 42–43

M
Maned wolves, 36
Mexico, 56, 131
Miacis, 26, *26*
Middle East, 39, 42, 59
Moose, 71–72, *72*, 122

N
National parks, 118, 121, 126–129
Native Americans
  Bella Coola, 13
  Hopi, 19
  Navajo, 19
  perceptions of wolves, 19–20, *20*
  Plains Indians, 20, *20*
North America, 32, 35, 40, 41

O
Offspring, 31, *31*, 85, 94, *95*, 96, *97*, 98, 99, *99*
  aardwolf, 36
  Canis rufus, 35
  coyotes, 38
  dingoes, 40
  dogs, 40
  foxes, 41–42
  jackals, 39
  maned wolf, 36
  Tasmanian wolf, 37, *37*
Oxen, musk, 74, *74*

P
Play, 78, *80–81*, 94, *95*, 98, *99*, 110, *112–113*
Poisoning, 17, 106, 108, 109, 126
Population control, 12

Prey. *See* Diet.
Proteles cristatus, 36

R
Rabbits, 72
Rabies, 13
Red wolves, *34*, 35, 132, *133*, *134*, 135
Reintroduction efforts, 35, 116–135

S
Scent marking, 76, 77
Senses
  hearing, 28, 77
  smell, 28, 67, 76–77
  vision, 77
Sheep, 74
Sociability, 12, 29, 54, 84–85, 88
  aardwolf, 36
  Canis lupus, 32
  Canis rufus, 35
  coyotes, 38
  dingoes, 40
  dogs, 40
  dominance and subordination in, 21, 84–85, 88
  foxes, 41–42
  and hierarchy, 84
  jackals, 39
  maned wolf, 36
  Tasmanian wolf, 37, *37*
South America, 36, 41, 43
Speothos venaticus, 43
Status
  Canis lupus, 32, 116–129
  Canis rufus, 35
  coyotes, 38
  dingoes, 40
  dogs, 40
  foxes, 41–42
  jackals, 39
  maned wolf, 36
  Tasmanian wolf, 37, *37*
Survival, 12, 52, 64, 66, 78. *See also* Diet.

T
Tasmanian wolves, 37, *37*
Territoriality, 28
Thylacinus cynocephalus, 36
Trapping, 39, 42, 106, 108, 122, 125

U
United States, 35, 38, 55–56, 118–121, *120*
Urocyon cinereoargenteus, 41–42

V
Vulpes vulpes, 40–41

W
Wapiti, 71
Werewolves, 13, *14*, 16, 21
Wolf children, 12, *12*
Wolf Summit, 122, 124, 125